CADILLAC

· T · H · E ·

Enduring Legend

CADILLAC

·T·H·E·

Enduring Legend

GALLERY BOOKS
An Imprint of W. H. Smith Publishers Inc.
112 Madison Avenue
New York City 0016

DEDICATION

For Gene Asbury and Fred Engle, whose help made this book possible. And to all Cadillac owners – my sincere thanks.

ACKNOWLEDGMENT

The publishers gratefully acknowledge the invaluable assistance provided by the following individuals and organizations throughout the preparation of this book:

Ron Root; Roy and Barb Hathaway; Fitzgerald Cadillac, Fort Wayne, Indiana; Gene and Magdalena Ashbury; Fred and Sidney Engle; J.S. and Wilma Plummer; Carl Riggins; Ed Oberhaus; Emmet Lawrence; Herb Rothman; Ted Davidson; Ralph Barbato; Mr. and Mrs. Paul Helton; Chip Baldoni, Betty Boop's Used Cars, Santa Fe Springs, California; Frank Ormonde; Joel Frescott; Unique Color Lab, Fort Wayne, Indiana; Jack's Camera Shop, Muncie, Indiana; Donna Begley; Don Reel; Larry Fitch; Sue and Richard O'Mara.

CLB 2351
© 1989 Colour Library Books Ltd., Godalming, Surrey, England.
This edition published in 1989 by Gallery Books,
an imprint of W.H. Smith Publishers, Inc.,
112 Madison Avenue, New York, 10016
Color separation by Scantrans Pte Ltd., Singapore.
Printed and bound in Italy by New Interlitho.
All rights reserved
ISBN 0 8317 1120 5

Gallery Books are available for bulk purchase for sales promotions and premium use. For details write or telephone the Manager of Special Sales, W.H. Smith Publishers, Inc.,
112 Madison Avenue, New York, New York 10016. (212) 532-6600

INTRODUCTION

Sometime in the last years of the seventeenth century a new settlement sprang up alongside the huge inland waterway of Lake Erie. The man responsible was a French military officer in charge of a small expeditionary force and a band of Indian guides. It was at his behest that this little group found itself on Lake Erie's west shore, for LeSieur Antoine de la Mothe Cadillac was of noble birth and his aristocratic background gave him the approval of King Louis XIV to explore and settle this vast and unspoiled continent of the Americas.

Little did Antoine Cadillac know what fate had decreed for the settlement they christened Ville d'Etroit; after all, there was nothing really special about the name – all it meant was "Village of the Straits." Nor could he have been aware how his proud name would eventually be used. The village became the industrial center of the Midwest, the capital of the car. Ville d'Etroit became Detroit, and Antoine de la Mothe Cadillac was immortalized in the annals of history when his name and coat of arms were taken to give dignity and class to a new automobile. From the time the first Cadillac took to the road, the name of the great French explorer became synonymous with quality the world over.

Henry Leland, Cadillac's founder and guiding light in the marque's early years, and his son, Wilfred, ran a successful machine tool business in Detroit. Obsessed with uncompromisingly high standards in precision toolmaking, the Lelands soon came to the notice of the fledgling motor industry – in particular, Ransom E. Olds, creator of the Oldsmobile. Olds needed a quieter, better transmission than the one he currently used and Leland came up with exactly what he required. Much impressed, Olds contracted Leland, Faulconer and Norton to build him 2,000 engines for his popular Curved Dash Olds. Like the transmission, Leland's single-cylinder engine was a shining example of precision fit, so good that any single part of any engine would fit another – an advantage almost unheard of in those days.

Unfortunately, high standards, in what was otherwise still a crude industry, cost money, and, when presented with the bill, Ransom E. Olds cited delays in production and any other excuse he could think of to cancel his order. Down, but by no means out, the Lelands returned to machine tool manufacturing.

But not for long. Henry Ford, one of the great motoring pioneers, was on the road to financial ruin. His Detroit Automobile Company was notable for its complete lack of success – and in 1903 he decided to go his own way, setting up the Ford Motor Company. Faced with the decision of whether to close down or not, the remaining directors of the Detroit Automobile Company called in Henry Leland to appraise the company's stock

Meanwhile, Leland had placed one of his cast-aside engines into his personal Oldsmobile and ran it as a sort of test bed. By this time he had convinced himself that motor manufacture was the way to go, and when Detroit Automobile Company officers came knocking on his door he realized here was a wonderful opportunity to start an

automobile business.

To cut a long story short – it is a long one and anybody interested should read Maurice Hendry's superb and definitive work, *Cadillac, Standard of the World* – Henry Leland persuaded the Detroit directors not to close down but to continue building the car they had begun. They wouldn't need worry about engines. Didn't he, Henry Leland, already have a superior engine of proven quality? A deal

was struck. Leland was made a director and the first Cadillac, known as the Model A, was rolled out on 17th October, 1902.

The Cadillac name was chosen wisely as it was to turn out. Detroit had recently celebrated its 200th birthday, so what better name than Cadillac? With Antoine de la Mothe Cadillac's heritage, the name smacked of old-world class and elegance. Shortly afterwards, Cadillac's famous coat

Title page: as elegant now as it was then, the 1940 Cadillac Series 62 Coupe de Ville is as timeless as the sea itself. Previous pages: its look says it all – even in 1964 this Series 62 Coupe de Ville was king of the American luxury road. If your world was the world of the rich and famous, you drove to the beach party in this 1955 topless Series 62 (above).

7

of arms was designed and application for the crest to become a registered trademark was granted in 1906.

Cadillac built 2,497 Model As during 1903. Compared to today's complex machines they were very simple in execution. The engine was a single-cylinder, 9.7 bhp, horizontally-mounted unit capable of 30 mph! The rear wheels were chain driven and the planetary transmission had two forward speeds and one reverse. The cost, which included hickory wood wheels, pneumatic tires, two headlights and a taillight, was $750.

From its earliest beginnings, Cadillac's success was guaranteed. In 1908 Cadillac won the coveted Dewar Trophy, motoring's Nobel Prize, if you like. It all started in 1903 when an ambitious Englishman, Frederick S. Bennett of the Anglo-American Motor Car Company of London, recognized Cadillac's abilities and became the first agent for the marque outside the United States. Bennett's association with Cadillac was as successful as it was adventurous; to prove the car's worth Bennett entered it in competitions, such as hill climbs and long-distance runs.

In 1908, at Britain's new racing track at Brooklands, in Surrey, three Cadillacs were picked at random, completely disassembled, and the parts intermixed Under the watchful eyes of Royal Automobile Club officials the 2,163 components were reassembled and the Cadillacs were given a 500-mile run around the Brooklands circuit. They performed without fault and Cadillac became the first American car company to be given the Dewar Trophy, awarded for the interchangeability and standardization of parts – an idea unheard of in Britain at the time. Henceforth Cadillac would become "The Standard of the World," as its advertising proudly proclaimed.

In 1906 Cadillac introduced its first four-cylinder engine and, while the single-cylinder cars remained popular, in 1909 Cadillac brought out a new, refined four-cylinder engine rated at 25.6 bhp. Only one model was made available in three styles. Although different styles later became available, Cadillac continued to be powered by the four-cylinder engine until 1915; by 1913 this engine had been bored out to 365.8 cubic inches and was rated at 48.7 horsepower!

The enigmatic William Crapo Durant wanted Cadillac in his newly formed motor group. Up until then it consisted of two struggling companies: Buick and Oldsmobile. Cadillac would be the standard-bearer, the flagship of General Motors.

The price was high, but Billy Durant succeeded in capturing Cadillac. Along with the purchase he also got the Lelands and Cadillac's complete management staff – conditions he had to agree if he wanted the car. A deal was struck and, in 1909, Cadillac became part of what eventually would be the largest industrial complex in the world.

Also in 1909, the Dayton Engineering Laboratories Co, run by the inventive genius Charles Kettering, signed a contract with Cadillac to produce a new starter system. The result was the world's first electric starter which revolutionized the automobile world, and won Cadillac its second Dewar Trophy in 1913, a feat not achieved by any other make, before or since.

Perhaps more so than any other car in those early days, Cadillac was the product of brilliant minds. As its advertising continually claimed, Cadillac had truly become "The Standard of the World," a claim the company did not flaunt lightly. Remember, Henry Leland was still very much at the helm and, in 1910, was getting anxious at Billy Durant's uncontrollable zeal for acquisition. It soon became apparent that Durant had over-extended General Motors'

none-too-tight coffers. This resulted in the bankers refusing any more loans and Durant being forced to leave the company he founded.

With Durant gone, General Motors reorganized and prospered. In 1915 Cadillac sprang yet another surprise on an unsuspecting world with the presentation of the first mass-produced V8. Known as the Type 51, the unit displaced 314 cubic inches and was rated at 70 bhp. Very smooth and silent, this revolutionary engine was capable of 65 mph, and Cadillac built 13,000 of them in its first year.

Billy Durant returned to take over GM again in 1916. By 1917 Leland and Durant were worlds apart – Leland wanted to build Liberty aero engines for America's war effort and Durant wanted no part of it. So Leland left, got an order for 6,000 aero engines and eventually created another great car. Still with us today, the Lincoln commands great respect as Ford's flagship.

Even without Leland, Cadillac continued to prosper. As the Twenties broke, there were numerous makes clambering for a place in the luxury bed. At the time, Packard was still regarded as *the* car to which to aspire, but Cadillac was gradually making inroads. Slowly but surely, Cadillac would reach the top of the heap, helped on its way by the introduction of the LaSalle, in 1927, and the monumental and exciting V12 and V16 engines in 1930/31. Covered in chrome, aluminum, porcelain and enamel, both these overhead valve engines were designed by Owen Nacker and were works of art in their own right. No hoses or wiring were be to seen, as these unsightly items were all tucked away under cover.

1937 appeared to be the last year for such a mammoth powerplant. Only fifty V16 ohv units a year had been built for 1934. Yet instead of dropping multi-cylinder engines, regarded as a bit of an anachronism by most people, especially during the Depression years, Cadillac dropped the ohv version and trotted out an entirely new L-head V16 in 1938. Lighter, yet not so refined to look at, the new engine could do everything its predecessor did – and perhaps a little more besides.

By 1940 Cadillac had reached the top of the luxury tree. Peerless, Marmon, Duesenberg, Pierce-Arrow, all were gone. Packard and Lincoln had fallen behind, and Cadillac's 1940/41 designs eclipsed Lincoln's magnificent V12 Continental. Then came the war and there would be no new development from Cadillac until 1948.

And that is where this book really begins. From 1946 to date Cadillac's story has been a continuing saga of improvement and innovation, some glorious, some inglorious. As far as style goes, the marque has gone from one extreme to the other; from the conservative to the flamboyant in one generation. As we approach the last decade of this fascinating, troubled century, Cadillac's mystique, its quality and, most of all, its individuality, have taken a step backward. More Lincolns are being sold than ever before and, unless Cadillac does something to reverse the trend, America will have a new luxury car king.

1989 models reflect a change for the better, however, and GM designers point to 1992 as the year when Cadillac will once again be crowned "Standard of the World." In the meantime, bathe yourselves in nostalgia, remember the fins of the Fifties; Elvis' pink '56; the glorious 1967 front-wheel drive; the monstrous 500-cubic-inch engine – the days, in fact, when Cadillac was truly king.

Facing page: a back road far from California's highway mayhem. This 1973 Coupe de Ville's suspension would sop up any bumps with aplomb.

1947-1959

With the surrender of Japan on August 15th, 1945 the Second World War finally came to an end. Two months later, on October 17, 1946, the first post-war Cadillac automobile emerged into the sunlight of a new beginning.

Cadillac had entered the war at the zenith of its hard-won reputation as the epitome of the American Dream. Hard won because it had to climb to the top in competition with the likes of Packard, Lincoln, Imperial, Marmon, Pierce-Arrow, Duesenberg and many others worthy of mention, not forgetting the luxury cars from Britain and Europe as well. This envious reputation was achieved through innovation, quality and driveability. Coupling the electric self starter in 1912, the first mass produced V8 in 1915 and then the fabulous V16 of the Thirties with its stylish coachwork and graceful lines, it is clear why Cadillac succeeded while others failed.

In a way, the war was an advantage, not because Cadillac had performed its patriotic duty like other car manufacturers and built thousands of much-needed tanks and guns, but because no new models had appeared for over three-and-a-half years, thus prompting over 100,000 orders for new Cadillac cars when the war ended. In other words, Cadillac still symbolized the American dream.

Major rivals were few – just Packard, Lincoln and sometimes Chrysler's Imperial – on the odd occasions when it was classed as a separate make and not a New Yorker with frills. The Depression had wiped out many grand marques, and mismanagement had accounted for the rest, so the burden of remaining at the top wasn't as difficult as it might have been. Still, there was the sister division, Buick. Not to be trusted, this toothy lot from Flint. Hadn't Buick tried to wrest Cadillac's favored position for itself? Fortunately, talk of Buick's standing in certain quarters of the British Royal Family fell on deaf ears in GM's corporate hierarchy; in fact, Buick was slapped down for even daring to suggest it was a better car than Cadillac!

Only 1,142 cars were built by Cadillac in 1945 and these were strictly warmed-over versions of the 1942 models, as were 1946 and 1947 Cadillacs, having little to distinguish them save slightly heavier grille bars and bumpers that wrapped around the corners for better protection. Eleven models in four series were offered, consisting of the Series 61, 62, 60, and 75. Lowest priced was the 61, the five-passenger coupe with a base price of $2,022, while the most expensive production Cadillac was the Series 75 seven-passenger sedan, retailing at $4,415 – only 225 were built for 1946.

By far the most attractive 1946 model was the Series 62 Convertible Coupe. $2,521 bought this car, but to make it worthwhile the buyer just had to have the Hydra-Matic transmission at $176.47, and full-size wheel discs and radio for a further $100. On a wheelbase of 129 inches and an overall length of 220 inches, this convertible was no small fry, but the ideal vehicle in which to fantasize about a moon lit trip on a warm summer's night with Rita Hayworth by your side.

All models were powered by the same battle-hardened

Nobody seemed to mind that the early postwar cars were warmed-over 1942 models; this 1947 Cadillac Series 62 convertible (left) was no exception. Note the "Sombrero" wheel discs. These became a popular option and quite a fad during the late Forties.

SPECIFICATIONS 1947

Series 61 (wb 126.0)		Weight	Price	Production
6107	club cpe	4,080	2,200	3,395
6109	sdn 4d	4,165	2,324	5,160
Series 62 (wb 129.0)				
6207	club cpe	4,145	2,446	7,245
6267	conv cpe	4,455	2,902	6,755
6269	sdn 4d	4,235	2,523	25,834
62	chassis	—	—	1
Series 60 Special (wb 133.0)				
6069	sdn 4d	4,370	3,195	8,500
Series 75 (wb 136.0)				
7519	sdn 4d	4,875	4,471	300
7523	sdn 4d, 7P	4,895	4,686	890
7523L	business sdn 9P	4,790	4,368	135
7533	imperial sdn 7P	4,930	4,887	1,005
7533L	business imperial sdn 9P	4,800	4,560	80
75	chassis	—	—	3
75	comm & bus chassis (wb 163.0)	—	—	2,623

1947 Engine	bore × stroke	bhp	availability
V8, 346.0	3.50 × 4.50	150	S-all

The lines of the 1947 Series 62 convertible (these pages) were a Harley Earl trademark. The front end (facing page top) is every bit a Cadillac, while pontoon fenders (below) had their beginnings in a Rubens painting.

346-cubic-inch L-head V8 – battle-hardened because it had successfully been used to power Cadillac's M-5 and M-24 tanks. Each tank was driven by two of these engines coupled to GM's Hydra-Matic transmissions. Knowing what sticklers the military are for trouble-free, durable machinery, Cadillac was able to refine and hone both engines and transmissions to a degree not possible under normal circumstances, so anyone buying a 1946/47 Cadillac automobile was buying a product which was the state of the art.

Total Cadillac production for 1946 was 29,194 cars. The most popular model was the Series 62 four-door Sedan, with 14,900 units produced. At the other end of the scale were the Series 75 four-door Imperial Sedan and four-door Business Imperial Sedan – only seventeen of each were built.

Although Cadillac came to be recognized as the luxury leader, Packard sales for 1946 were actually higher, totalling 30,883. Slightly over half this total was for the mid-priced Clipper Six models; take away the Clipper Sixes and Cadillac was way out in front. Nevertheless, regardless of size or price, it should not be forgotten that Packard was once referred to as "America's Rolls-Royce."

Detroit had never had it so good. As 1947 rolled round, America's appetite for new cars became insatiable. The post-war economy was booming, everybody had money and everybody wanted a new car to replace the weary pre-war models limping sadly to the scrap yard. No matter that the new cars were virtually the same as the pre-war ones – nobody cared. The paint was shiny, the chrome was bright – the cars were new, and that's all that mattered.

A few cosmetic changes heralded Cadillac's 1947 crop. Instead of six die-cast metal bars, the new grille had five

stamped ones. Heavier than before, the bars extended into the graceful pontoon front fender, while the rear pontoons were given a stainless-steel stone shield in place of the rubber one used the previous year. One styling change of note was the inclusion of "Sombrero" full-size wheel covers. At $25.08 a set, these covers rapidly became popular and were soon copied by the rest of the industry. As far as series, models and mechanical specifications went, everything remained as 1947 except prices – they went up.

Before the war, especially during the early to mid Thirties, custom coach-builders proliferated on the American automotive landscape. By 1947, however, most of these had disappeared. Only Derham remained to build the odd formal limousine conversions of Fleetwood 75 models. Some of these were attractive in a stately sort of way and certainly would have been quite at home hauling some king or president from one function to another. As for those who wished to take their last ride in a Cadillac, the Hess and Eisenhardt Company of Cincinnati did a nice line in Cadillac funeral cars and hearses for a company known as Sayers and Scovill, who sold these and other specialized Cadillac products to funeral homes.

Production, at 61,926 units, was more than double that of the previous year and Cadillac still had back orders totalling 96,000 cars. As 1947 wound down, Cadillac was busily getting itself ready for its next stage of post-war development. An all-new Cadillac was about to take its bow, a Cadillac that really would usher in the dawn of a new age.

It had all begun before the war with Harley J. Earl, the son of a Los Angeles-based carriage maker. Educated at Stanford University, young Harley soon showed his artistic talents, first at his father's carriage works and then later at the Don Lee Cadillac agency. Lee's agency sold cars to the stars, and because Holywood types wanted to be noticed and be seen to be different, Don Lee employed Harley to do custom coachwork.

It was on one of his tours of California Cadillac dealerships that Lawrence P. Fisher, Cadillac's general manager, visited the Don Lee Agency, where he met Harley Earl. He was interested to see the special bodies the tall young man had created for Hollywood's rich and famous, and he was impressed with what he saw. Once back in Detroit, Fisher persuaded GM head, Alfred P. Sloan, to try Earl out on some Cadillac projects in the works.

The outcome of Earl's introduction to Detroit was the 1927 LaSalle. Even though it had shades of Hispano-Suiza in its design, the LaSalle was a triumph of artistry at a time when cars were mostly unimaginative and boxy. At the behest of a much-impressed Sloan, Harley Earl set up the world's first styling studio in 1927. Thus GM's famous Art and Color Design section began with the youthful Harley Earl as its head.

Pearl Harbor and the beginning of America's involvement in WW II was still a long way off on the day Harley Earl and others of his design team saw the still-top-secret Lockheed Lightning P-38 fighter. Earl marveled at the airplane's shape, particularly its slender twin booms ending in vertical "tails." Other aspects of the aircraft intrigued him enough to

Every bit the Standard of the World it claimed to be, Cadillac's 1949 Coupe de Ville (right) featured the world's first hardtop styling (along with sisters Oldsmobile Holiday and Buick Riviera), an advanced new OHV V8, graceful lines and those unique tail fins.

14

1949 CADILLAC SERIES 62 COUPE DE VILLE

SPECIFICATIONS
1949

Series 61 (wb 126.0)		Weight	Price	Production
6107	club cpe	3,838	2,788	6,409
6169	sdn 4d	3,915	2,893	15,738
61	chassis	—	—	1
Series 62 (wb 126.0)				
6207	club cpe	3,862	2,966	7,515
6237	Coupe de Ville htp cpe	4,033	3,497	2,150
6267	conv cpe	4,218	3,442	8,000
6269	sdn 4d	3,956	3,050	37,977
62	chassis	—	—	1
Series 60 Special (wb 133.0)				
6037	Coupe de Ville htp cpe	4,200	exp	1
6069	sdn 4d	4,129	3,828	11,399
Series 75 (wb 136.0)				
7519	sdn 4d	4,579	4,750	220
7523	sdn 4d, 7P	4,626	4,970	595
7523L	business sdn 9P	4,522	4,650	35
7533	imperial sdn 7P	4,648	5,170	626
7533L	business imperial sdn 9P	4,573	4,839	25
75	chassis	—	—	1
86	comm chassis (wb 163.0)	—	—	1,861

1949 Engine	bore × stroke	bhp	availability
V8, 331.0	3.81 × 3.63	160	S-all

Top: the three-piece rear window was a design feature on some Cadillac models through 1953. Above: top quality leather and cloth interiors enhanced Cadillac's stature. Facing page: the attractive 1940 advertisement is anything but subtle.

Jewels by Harry Winston

Cadillac

ILLUSTRATED HERE is the Coupe de Ville—a smart new Cadillac body type, designed for those who seek the low-swept lines and open-airiness of a convertible—combined with the comfort, convenience and safety of a closed car. It is a classic example of modernity and practicality —one of the most desirable and most useful models ever to issue from the boards of Cadillac designers. Yet—smart and beautiful as it is— its greatest superiority lies in the chassis on which it is built. For, like a Cadillac, the core of its goodness is found in its *performance* —in the wonderful capacity of its new V-type engine; in the soft, even, restful manner in which it rolls over the highway; in the easy, effortless response to steering wheel and brakes. It is, truly, a symphony in motion. Your Cadillac dealer will be pleased to give you full details about this wonderful new body type—as well as the other beautiful models which grace his showroom.

★ CADILLAC MOTOR CAR DIVISION ★ GENERAL MOTORS CORPORATION ★

1949

17

consider adapting certain of the P-38's features to an automobile.

That automobile was the 1948 Cadillac.

When the first true post-war Cadillac was launched in 1948, it was late. Production didn't start until February 1948, due to extensive retooling measures. So it wasn't until March that the new car finally hit dealers' showrooms. It was startling, it was controversial, it was beautiful. Little of the past remained; this new Cadillac had wiped the slate clean. It was Space Age, but it was no work of fiction. It was as real as the plane that inspired it.

Only six of Cadillac's eleven models were graced with the new design: the Series 60, 61, and 62 cars. For some reason the Series 75 continued as before, leading one to think this was done to appease the more conservative elements who might be resistant to sudden change.

Obviously the most prominent feature of Cadillac's design were the tailfins – small appendages contradicting the downward flow of the rear pontoon-style fenders, breaking away on their own, yet perfectly integrated in the overall design. The tips of the tailfins, rudders, fish-tails, call them what you will, carried beautifully-blended taillights – the left taillight popped up at the touch of a small reflector to reveal the gas filler, a novel touch if ever there was one. Another nice touch was the rear bumper, its extremities neatly housed in the rear fender, just below the finned taillights.

At the front, the new grille was a variation of Cadillac's eggcrate theme, prevalent since 1941. With only three horizontal bars attached to seven vertical ones, the grille accentuated Cadillac's fleet, low design. A much-improved glass area was assisted by thin "A" pillars, while the curved windshield comprised two sections divided by a bar in the middle.

The hood line was flatter and the car appeared longer due to its slab sides, which extended uninterrupted to the rear fender pontoon. Of the various models offered, the Series 61 and Series 62 fastback coupes were by far the most attractive Cadillacs for 1948, even though the four-door sedans outsold them three-and-a-half to one.

Underneath all the glitter was familiar territory, save the new shock absorber valves and springs. Front independent suspension geometry was slightly altered for improved caster and camber, while the channel section steel frame had a center X member for better rigidity. The weight for a complete car averaged approximately 4,160 pounds. There was nothing new under the hood, either – just the same old L-head Cadillac had been using since 1936, displacing 346 cubic inches and developing 150 bhp. However, as we shall see, there were changes in the pipeline that would revolutionize American engine development.

Due to the Cadillac's late 1948 introduction, only 52,706 cars were produced for the model year. As far as public acceptance was concerned, though, the radical new styling was enthusiastically received even though it took a couple of months to gain acceptance, much in the same way that the Taurus, the Sable and England's Ford Sierra were gradually accepted.

Three men: Harry F. Barr, Edward N. Cole and John F. Gordon, were responsible for Cadillac's technological leap

Cadillac's 75 series (right) had to wait until 1950 before its prewar body was retired in favor of new styling.

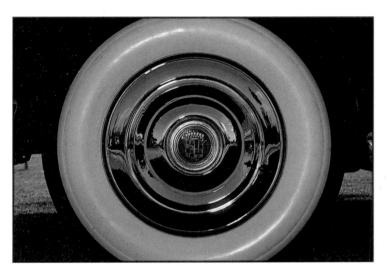

Top: heavy metal grille stamping denotes a quality that is sadly missed today. Above center: the smart "Sombrero" wheel cover is a collector's item in itself. Above: the rear of the car's interior features Bedford cord upholstery, real wood cappings and more room than a dance hall. Right: an extremely attractive car, the Fleetwood Series 75 saw a 1949 production total of only 1,801 split between five models.

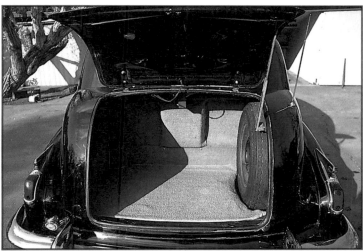

Top: the 75 limousine's attractive taillight cleverly hides the gas filler, while its spacious trunk (above) will carry more than today's full size Brougham. Right: considering the glass is almost flat, the three-window effect is nothing more than a styling ploy. Chromed extension trunk hinges show that the car is a prewar design. Overleaf: the Series 62 convertible had a production run of 8,000 units in 1949, yet only 2,150 of the new Coupe de Ville hardtops were built.

forward in 1949. During the late Thirties Barr, who was Cadillac's staff engineer in charge of engine design, Cadillac Chief Engineer Ed Cole, and Cadillac Division General Manager John Gordon, began development work on a brand-new V8 engine. Incidentally, it is worth noting that the "General" had a knack for hiring extremely talented people who often remained with the company until retirement. A case in point was the hiring of Barr, Cole and Gordon. Barr went on to become GM Engineering Vice President, while Cole and Gordon both rose to the presidency of GM – at different times, of course!

1949 was the year Chrysler would slip back to third place behind Ford, who came out with striking new cars equipped with independent front suspension – a first for the Dearborn company whose technology had so far lagged behind the rest of the industry. Yet it was Cadillac and Oldsmobile who did most of the leaping that year with brand new V8s. Both engines were overhead valve designs and were built independently of each other.

A quick word about Oldsmobile's "Rocket 88", as it would become known. It was designed by Gilbert Burrell, displaced 303 cubic inches, had five main bearings, an over-square bore and stroke of 3.75 x 3.44 inches, and developed 135 bhp at 3,600 rpm. Considerably lighter and more flexible than the in-line side-valve eight it replaced, Olds' V8 had a compression ratio of 7.25:1, but, anticipating higher octane fuel, the engineers designed the engine to have ratios as high as 12:1. As every auto-mad kid on the block soon knew, Olds dropped the engine into its lightweight 88 models. In this guise Oldsmobile became the car to beat on the NASCAR tracks and can be said to have been a progenitor of the muscle car.

As for Cadillac's startling new V8, there *were* differences,

even if the overriding philosophy was the same. It was larger than Oldsmobile's, displacing 331 cubic inches and putting out 160 bhp. It employed unique "slipper" pistons, and its lower sides were cut away to enable the pistons to come to rest between the crankshaft counterweights at the end of the stroke. One of its advantages was its ability to use shorter connecting rods than the norm, thus helping to reduce the engine's size and weight. In fact, the new V8 weighed 221 lbs less than the L-head it replaced.

It is said that over one million miles of tests were conducted before the engine was approved for production. Cadillac wanted to ensure its reputation stayed intact and a less-than-perfect engine wouldn't help. By the time the engine appeared in the 1949 Cadillacs, it was as perfect as it could be – in fact it stayed in production until 1968, its versatility proven by the various modifications carried out through the years. By 1967, the block had been bored out to 429 cubic inches, attesting to the fact that this short-stroke, high-compression unit was one of the finest V8s ever built.

In a move designed to slug the competition (Lincoln had an all-new model for 1949), Cadillac made hay by introducing the 1949 Cadillacs halfway through 1948. This also took care of Packard's first post-war car, which came out as a '48 model. Poor Packard. As if Cadillac's 1948 styling wasn't enough to contend with, now there was a new V8 as well! At the end of the 1949 year, Cadillac had

Top: the Cadillac's overly-large steering wheel was made from an early form of plastic. Facing page: almost an art form, the front of the 1949 Series 62 was a simple yet successful blend of shapes. Overleaf: the 1953 Eldorado convertible; Cadillac and Harley Earl surpassed themselves with this ultra luxurious, low production automobile.

1953 CADILLAC ELDORADO CONVERTIBLE

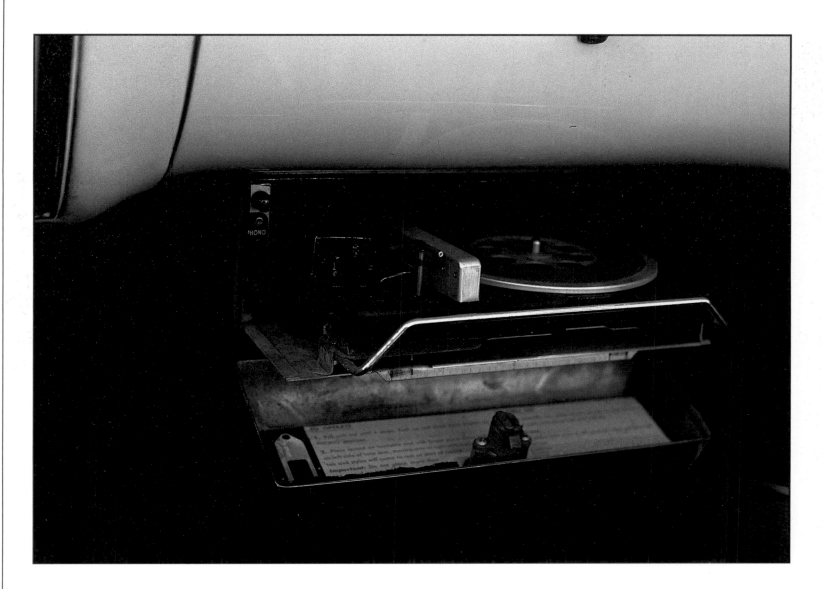

chalked up record sales of 92,554 cars against Packard's creditable 63,817. After all, Cadillac had had several months start – probably the difference in sales would have been far less had both sides begun their model runs at the same time.

Styling for the 1949 Cadillacs was much the same, but to take advantage of the four-inch-lower engine and and the correspondingly lower radiator, the grille was extended into the fenders, while the parking lights and center grille bar wrapped round the corners of the fenders to the front wheel arches. Other than this, there was little external difference to distinguish 1948 from 1949, with one exception – the hardtop.

Had it not been for the new engine, Cadillac's pillarless two-door hardtop would have been the big news. By pillarless we mean there were no side pillars – once the windows were down, the car was like a convertible with a steel roof. It was a beautiful car, and with a production of only 2,150, the Cadillac Series 62 Coupe de Ville hardtop is one of the most desired collector cars of the Forties. At the end of 1949, both Buick and Oldsmobile had hardtop models, a styling feature that was to remain until the Seventies.

Ninety-eight percent of Cadillac's customers specified Hydra-Matic automatic transmission in 1948 and 1949, and as time went on it would be the only transmission available in America's top car. By 1950 the four-speed automatic was standard in the Cadillac Fleetwood 60 Special and on Series 62 models, while the three-speed manual became an increasingly rare feature on all other series.

1950 heralded a period of political insecurities within the United States. Cadillac, however, remained aloof to the situation, concentrating instead on building 100,000 cars for the 1950 model year. This was achieved on November 16, 1950 and the year ended with Cadillac setting a new production record of 103,857 cars. This was one of many sales records Cadillac was to post over the next forty years. On November 25th of the previous year, the one-millionth Cadillac had been built – this after forty-seven years of automobile production. The way things looked, the second million would be built four times as fast!

Cadillac entered the second half of the twentieth century with a complete restyle of all its models. The fastback/sedanette bodystyle was gone and the two-door hardtop coupe filled the empty space in the Series 61 lineup. This series was unique thanks to its use of a 122-inch wheelbase for the first time; previously it had shared the 126-inch wheelbase with the Series 62 line. Due to its smaller wheelbase, the 61 Series was about two-and-a-quarter inches shorter overall than 1949, but the 62 went up almost two inches. As for the Series 60, this was down three inches to a 130-inch wheelbase, but the Series 75 – which did not adopt the new post-war styling until 1950 – had a wheelbase of 146.75 inches and an overall length of 235.575 inches.

All Cadillacs were big, but the Fleetwood 75 Series was gargantuan. Push the rear jump seats out of the way and there seemed enough room to hold a ballroom dancing competition! Occupants of these cars either imagined they were – or else they actually were – somebody

Top left: $7,750 was a lot of money back in 1953, but the new Eldorado came with every single convenience known to automotive man. The record player (top), however, was an after market option. Facing page: the car's massive grille had more chrome even than the more recent Broughams.

important. Limousines had black leather seating and mottled leather carpeting up front, while the VIPs in the rear reclined in soft Bedford cord or broadcloth upholstery. Incredibly, the standard transmission was the three-speed manual, but this would change in the very near future.

Heavier and more aggressive was Cadillac's shape for the beginning of the Fifties. The grille followed the same theme as 1948/49, but was chunkier, more massive and came to a rounded point at the center. The hood appeared higher, possibly due to the heavier profile, accentuated by the uninterrupted fender line flowing gracefully to a conclusion at the lip of the now-famous tailfins. A phony chromium vertical "airscoop" slashed down the leading edge of the rear fender and the upper grille bar continued on its merry way as a sweep spear into the front doors. A heavy-duty "V" hood emblem protected Cadillac's crest and was repeated on the trunk lid. Series 62 Cadillacs had a bright sill molding running from the back of the squared front wheel arch along the rear fender skirts to the bumper.

An area not normally considered Cadillac territory is competition, yet in 1950 Cadillac went racing in various guises. The British sportscar designer Sydney Allard fitted the new V8 into his Allards and successfully raced them against Ferrari and Jaguar. Meanwhile, wealthy American Briggs Cunningham took two Cadillacs to France and competed in the Le Mans 24-hour race. One car was a completely stock Series 61 coupe, the other, an extraordinary concoction christened "Le Monstre" by the French crowds. This car was an early attempt at aerodynamics and the body was fitted to a standard Cadillac chassis. Both cars did extremely well, the stock Series 61 finishing tenth overall, with "Le Monstre" in eleventh place. This was really the first and last time Cadillac took to the sporting arena – the

nearest it got to anything sporty, apart from Allard, was if the engines were transplanted into hot rods.

All things considered, the 1950 Cadillac was pure artistry of design. From its massive grille to its three-piece curved window, Cadillac was a powerful statement of what it meant to be successful – in short, the crowning glory of the American Dream.

1951 gave Cadillac another record sales year, with 110,340 cars sold. After a total restyle the previous year, 1951 Cadillacs contented themselves with a new bumper design, highlighted by the largest Jayne Mansfield-type projections yet seen on an automobile. On May 1st, 1951, Cadillac's Series 61 was dropped due to low sales – there had been only 4,700 Series 61 cars since the beginning of the year. Remember: no matter how good you are, you don't get breaks in Detroit: if you don't sell, you get the bullet!

All other Cadillac series remained as before, the 331-cubic-inch V8 still pushing out 160 horsepower. However, it was Chrysler's turn to drop a well-designed bombshell. It chose 1951 to launch its fantastic hemispherical combustion chamber ohv V8. In one fell swoop it just about wiped out the opposition – not in sales terms, but certainly in advanced engine technology. Displacing the same 331 cubic inches as Cadillac's V8, Chrysler's famed "Hemi-head" took a commanding lead in the horsepower race, having 180 eager horses under the hood. This new engine attracted the attention of Briggs Cunningham, who eventually designed a race car round it, while America's leading automotive tester, Tom McCahill, had nothing but praise for it.

Chrysler's hemi launched the horsepower race with a bang, but Cadillac had no intention of staying the

underdog for long. 1952 was the marque's fiftieth anniversary
– the culmination of fifty years of unparallelled excellence
in design and innovative engineering. Even though it was
its fiftieth birthday, Cadillac celebrated the event modestly,
as one would expect of an aristocrat.

Apart from minor detail changes, Cadillac remained
the same as 1951 – in exterior detail, that is. It was under the
skin where several important changes occurred. The V8's
horsepower was increased to 190 and the unit was
equipped with a Rochester four-barrel Quadra Jet
downdraft carburetor. This was a first for the motor industry
and quite probably upset those at Chrysler and Lincoln –
especially as Buick and Oldsmobile also offered this
innovation. A new dual-range Hydra-Matic transmission
was made standard on all Cadillacs except the 75 Series,
offering the driver manual control on third and fourth gears
if desired. Another feature was the Saginaw power steering,
so far only offered as an option, and, judging by the weight
and size of these cars, was a much-needed option at that.

Only seven body styles were offered in three series for
1952: four in the popular 62 Series; one, a four-door sedan,
in the 60 Series; and two in the 75 Series, down from three in
1951. The year ended with a downward trend in sales to
90,259 units delivered. At least one small comfort was *Motor
Trend* magazine's "Car of the Year Award", given to Cadillac
for engineering excellence.

Into 1953 and again very little styling change; the "Jayne
Mansfield" bumper protectors looked less like Jayne
Mansfield and were moved up and toward the outer
extremities of the grille, where the parking/directional fog
lamps used to be. These in turn became part of the outer
grille extensions, beneath the headlights. New, plush interiors
graced all Cadillac models, while a novel option was the

SPECIFICATIONS
1953

Series 62 (wb 126.0)		Weight	Price	Production
62.9	sdn 4d	4,225	3,666	47,640
6237	cpe	4,320	3,571	14,353
6237D	Coupe de Ville htp cpe	4,320	3,995	14,550
62E7	conv cpe	4,500	4,144	8,367
62E7S	Eldorado conv cpe	4,800	7,750	532
62	chassis	—	—	4
Series 60 Special (wb 130.0)				
6019	sdn 4d	4,415	4,305	20,000
Series 75 (wb 146.8)				
7523	sdn 4d, 8P	4,830	5,408	1,435
7533	imperial sdn 8P	4,850	5,621	765
8680S	comm chassis (wb 157.0)	—	—	2,005

1953 Engine	bore × stroke	bhp	availability
V8, 331.0	3.81 × 3.63	210	S-all

*Facing page: there was nothing plastic about the '53
Eldorado's interior, in which top quality leather upholstery
cocooned the occupants. Above: set well back from the grille,
the Eldorado's engine looks mercifully easy to work on. Cadillac
only made 532 1953 Eldorados. The '54 model (overleaf),
though loaded, cost $2,000 less and, apart from unique
extension trim, had styling identical to standard Caddie
convertibles.*

"Autronic Eye". This space-age sensor, which automatically dimmed the headlights for approaching traffic, was mounted on top of the dashboard to the left of the instrument panel. Much more important, though, was the introduction of air conditioning, supplied by GM's Frigidaire Division. This $619.55 option was a godsend for those in America's hotter regions and although it got off to a slow start, air conditioning would ultimately become a requirement on all cars.

America's horsepower race was mainly fueled by Cadillac, who pushed output up to 210 bhp in 1953, while Chrysler remained pat on 180. However, the latter had more things to worry about than horsepower races: sales were disappearing down the river and drab, old-hat styling was killing America's number three car company. To redress the balance, Chrysler called in stylist Virgil Exner to try and work a miracle.

One additional model graced Cadillac's 1953 stable – the exciting, beautifully-styled Eldorado convertible. A feature attraction at GM's annual Motorama jamborees, the Eldorado was Harley Earl's way of saying "GM builds the best and the best is Cadillac." Based on the Series 62 line, the Eldorado featured a wrap-around windshield, a flush-fitting metal boot that concealed the electrically operated top when it was down, and a waist-level dip in the door line that did not feature on any other Cadillacs.

Mechanically, the Eldorado was the same as other Cadillacs, but every luxury was standard equipment. Everything from wire wheels, Hydra-Matic transmission, leather upholstery, powered windows, seats and steering, a signal-seeking pre-selector radio, dual outside mirrors, front and rear heating, whitewall tires, anti-glare dashboard top and windshield washer – all these were standard at the hefty price of $7,750.

Although a specialist car in 1953, Eldorado would soon become a top-line production model. However, 1953 was its glory year, as the Eldorado was recognized as the top car by no less a personality than the new President of the United States, Dwight Eisenhower, who rode in one on the day of his inauguration. The year ended with Cadillac posting sales of 109,651 cars and, as such, 1953 was the second best year in its fifty-year history.

Passing almost unnoticed around this time – except by teenagers – was a movie called *Blackboard Jungle*, whose song "Rock Around the Clock" by Bill Haley was destined to be significant. It was a significant year for Cadillac, too. 1954 ushered in totally new restyling, the first in four years. Three series, the 62, 60, and 75, comprising eight models, featured lower, wider cars with three inches extra length added to their wheelbases and between one and three inches extra overall.

From the combined bumper/grille which featured a finely textured eggcrate design, to the taillights, the styling was all new, yet evolutionary. No Cadillac could be mistaken for anything else; rather like Rolls-Royce, Cadillac's distinction was its purity of design. Although the 1954 models met mixed reviews ("Uncle" Tom McCahill certainly didn't like it), Harley Earl's design would ultimately prove to be smack on target – a complete statement of its time.

From hood to trunk, the '54 Eldorado was every inch a Cadillac. The "Continental wheel kit" (above) was a popular add-on in the mid Fifties.

As it was so successfully used on the stunning Eldorado in 1953, all Cadillacs, Buicks and Oldsmobiles adopted the wrap-around windshield, but Cadillac led the way with their high, slab sides, an aggressive, thrusting hood, a graceful curve in the rear roofline where it met the new wrap-around back window and the finely textured, yet massive, grille incorporating the largest "Dagmar's" in the company's history. The name Dagmar was adopted to describe the bumper projections after a television actress whose physical attributes require no explanation. Twenty more horsepower were ladled out, bringing Cadillac's rating up to 230 at 4400 rpm. Compression now stood at 8.25:1, and it was advisable to use premium fuel. After rigorous tests, *Motor Trend* called Caddie the Top-Performing car of 1954, yet Chrysler's New Yorker was still the fastest, if only just.

Power steering and windshield washers became standard on all Cadillacs, and Hydra-Matic was finally made standard on the 75 Series. As for the Series 62, the Eldorado returned but was now a production-line automobile with little more than a broad chrome panel decorating the lower rear fenders to distinguish it. Gold crests on the door sills, a fiberglass convertible top cover, wire wheels and most options standard, brought the Eldo's price to a respectable $5,738 – a little over $2,000 less than in '53.

Only modest changes highlighted Cadillacs for 1955 and 1956, the exception being the Eldorado convertible, which was given an exclusive appearance with a rear fender line and fins different from all other models. Gone were the traditional fins, to be replaced by a sharper, chrome-capped design with twin taillight appendages jutting out of long pods running all the way back to the wheel arch. The whole effect was that of a Flash Gordon rocketship that had sunk up to its nacelles.

As everybody who has studied post-war American automotive history knows, 1955 was the year all auto sales records were broken: a staggering 7.9 million cars were built, and Cadillac contributed with an all-time record 140,777.

In 1956 Chrysler led the way in the horsepower race, its 300B putting out 355 bhp. Packard was next with 290 and 310, depending which model you bought, but Lincoln remained on an equal footing with Cadillac, both rated at 285. Only Eldorado got more power: 305 horses this time. Styling of 1956 Cadillacs changed little, but an option for those who wanted to be noticed was a gold anodized grille, and wheels too, if the car was the Eldorado.

Speaking of Eldorados, there were two in the 1956 lineup. The convertible was renamed the Eldorado Biarritz to make way for the new Seville two-door hardtop coupe. Both cars were in the popular 62 Series, which now boasted seven of Cadillac's ten body styles.

Although Cadillac chalked up a new model-year production total of 147,502 units, there were events happening outside Clark Avenue that might have caused a little unease. One was the sparkling new Lincoln Continental Mark II. Priced at a record $10,000, this new Continental was making a bid to capture the status crown. Almost hand-built, the Mark II was the envy of the world. Packard, however, were in trouble. Their previous year's styling had brought shades of former glory with a unique torsion bar suspension, new V8 engine and Ultramatic transmission, but unfortunately the company hadn't done its homework, and the '55 cars were plagued with troubles. By 1956 these had been ironed out, but the damage was done. Two years later Cadillac would have one less contender to worry about when Packard left the stage as nothing more than a luxury Studebaker.

1956 Cadillacs, although praised for their quality, were criticised by many in the automotive media, and these criticisms were often justified, especially when it came to handling and weight. For example, a 1948 Series 62 four-door sedan weighed 4,180 lbs, measured 214 inches overall and cost $2,996. By 1956 the weight had jumped 230 lbs to 4,430. Length was about the same, but price had leapt to $4,296. Don't let anybody kid you into thinking more weight aids handling – the opposite is true. Logic tells us weight distribution is very important when it comes to handling and braking. Mid-Fifties cars with too much weight over the front wheels tended toward erratic behavior if the brakes were applied – and no matter how sharp they looked, many American cars of the period had very poor brakes. Allied with squishy handling, these cars could be very

SPECIFICATIONS
1954

Series 62 (wb 129.0)		Weight	Price	Production
6219	sdn 4d	4,370	3,933	34,252
6219S	DeVille htp sdn	—	proto	1
6237	htp cpe	4,365	3,838	17,460
6237D	Coupe de Ville htp cpe	4,405	4,261	17,170
6267	conv cpe	4,610	4,404	6,310
6267S	Eldorado conv cpe	4,815	4,738	2,150
62	chassis	—	—	1
Series 60 Special (wb 133.0)				
6019	sdn 4d	4,500	4,863	16,200
Series 75 (wb 149.8)				
7523	sdn 4d, 8P	5,055	5,875	889
7533	imperial sdn 8P	5,105	6,090	611
8680S	comm chassis (wb 158.0)	—	—	1,635

1954 Engine	bore × stroke	bhp	availability
V8, 331.0	3.81 × 3.63	230	S-all

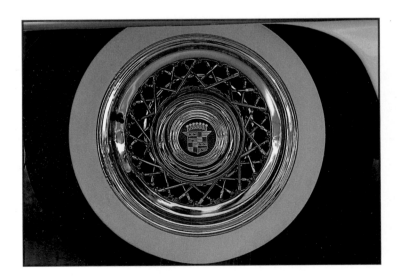

At $325 a set, not every Cadillac owner ordered the smart wire wheels (above). Facing page: cream and chrome trim on the Eldorado steering wheel echoes the car's exterior treatment. Overleaf: at a little over 216 inches overall, the 1954 Cadillac Series 62 sedan was the shortest model, and at $3,933 it was also the least expensive.

Facing page: "Sombrero" wheel covers (top left) were still a
Cadillac trademark in 1954, while the taillight (top right), which
popped open at the touch of a button to reveal the gas cap,
had been a Cadillac feature since 1948. Bottom: LeSieur
Antoine de la Mothe Cadillac's crest carries on a proud
tradition. Above: burgeoning bumper projections drew many
ribald comments.

1954 CADILLAC SERIES 62 4 DOOR SEDAN

unstable in inexperienced hands – perhaps that was why Elvis Presley's mother didn't drive the pink '56 her famous son bought her! Like most American cars of the day, Cadillacs were art on wheels and, as such, all form rather than function.

In the cut-throat car market of the Fifties, each manufacturer made a point of knowing what his rivals were up to. Cadillac was no exception and they knew, probably before many Ford executives knew, about the Continental Mark II. So, to answer the challenge, a program was put into operation on an even more expensive model than the one Lincoln had.

It was to be called the Eldorado Brougham and it was to debut in 1957.

Dramatic restyling announced Cadillac's entry into the motoring fray for 1957, but no matter how dramatic Cadillac may have been, Virgil Exner's 1957 Chrysler cars stole the show – and the styling leadership as well. In fact, all Chrysler marques, from the Plymouth to the Imperial, made all other cars look out of date. "Suddenly it's 1960," Chrysler's ads crowed – and it was.

Of course, Chrysler's competitors knew something special was in the works, so everybody – or almost everybody – tried to upstage Highland Park with a show of fins. Even Hudson had fins, albeit awkward add-ons, while the 1957 Ford crop had quite a good display. So did Cadillac, which lost its classic little appendages in the rush and ended up with something like a shark fin. Chrysler's fins, though, were magnificent – as much a part of each model as Hudson's weren't. Four inches less height, attractively sloped wrap-around windshields, and torsion bar front suspension gave them the best handling ever seen on an American car. Rival auto chiefs bit their corporate nails in anguish.

All this was too much for GM, whose styling leadership had been shot down in flames. A crash program was put into effect: fins for 1959 was the order of the day, and Cadillac was at the head of the list.

No matter that both Lincoln and Chrysler's beautiful Imperial – remember Jayne Mansfield's big white convertible in *The Girl Can't Help It*? – had massive sales gains, Cadillac still had an attractively styled automobile. Three inches lower than 1956 models thanks to a new tubular center X frame, all ten models had lower, flatter hoods and rear decks, wrap-around windshields that wrapped even further, rubber-tipped bumper protectors no less – my, my, what was the world coming to! – and a lower crosshatch grille that didn't say *Cadillac* with quite the same confidence as before. Hooded headlights and the aforementioned forward-sloping tail fins were complemented by the previous year's Eldorado's space-age taillights and a curious anomaly – a backward-sloped rear roof pillar that didn't quite make it. Razor-edged twin chrome wind splits adorned the hood where the graceful lady mascot used to be – the sort of ornamentation Ralph Nader would have had kittens over.

Both production Eldorados had different rear styling from other models. Shark-style fins jutted out of a smooth, very rounded rear quarter similar to the Corvette. Or a bee. Come to think of it, from the rear pillar back, both Eldos did have the look of a well-fed bee....

New Cadillac styling ably mirrored America's smug satisfaction at being "on top of the world" during the mid Fifties. Overleaf: sedate and sophisticated, the $4,683 Fleetwood 60 Special was perhaps the most handsome of all 1954 Cadillacs.

Gold anodised trim (facing page top) was a feature on all mid-Fifties Cadillacs. The hood ornament (facing page bottom) was a sign of better times. Above: the Cadillac front end – a work of stylist's art

All Cadillacs came with 300 bhp; 325 if they were Eldorados. The same 325 hp V8 was standard in the incredible, virtually hand-built Eldorado Brougham. Priced at a staggering $13,074, it was the most expensive Cadillac of all time and was up there with, if not ahead of, Rolls-Royce in terms of cost. As far as standard features went, the Brougham made Rolls-Royce look like a base Chevrolet. It had everything: powered windows, steering and brakes, a memory seat, an automatic trunk lid, power door locks and radio antenna, automatic engine starting, a complex air suspension system that invariably didn't work, anti-drive control, leather and brocade interiors and numerous other knick-knacks. With the ladies in mind, the Brougham had a tissue dispenser, a vanity compact, lipstick and perfume, and then there were four gold-finished, magnetic cups for morning coffee!

Although the Eldorado Brougham was a magnificent car, the fate of Ford's Continental Mark II should have warned Cadillac of things to come: only 3,012 examples of this exclusive automobile were sold and the model was consequently dropped after only twenty months' production. As for the Brougham, a mere 400 were produced in 1957 and only 304 in 1958. By 1959 this great experiment had gone the way of so many good things in America – to oblivion.

If Rolls-Royce can make a living building two or three thousand cars a year, why can't Ford or GM? Here are two companies with enormous resources, companies that could swallow R-R without even noticing it, and they can't – or won't – build an exclusive and very expensive car in small

numbers. Were they to do this, their prestige would rocket skyward and the cars *would* sell. After all, a Rolls Corniche sells for well over $100,000 and the company cannot supply enough. It's time Detroit did likewise – and the Allante isn't the answer!

After a record 154,577 cars built in 1956, Cadillac's 1957 and 1958 totals were a bit of an anti-climax: 146,841 and 121,778 respectively. If that was poor, think of Chrysler and Ford. Chrysler, whose sales broke records in 1957, let itself down with almost non-existent quality control. What do you do when the Imperial you buy has rust in the showroom, and a Plymouth's steering wheel comes off in your wife's hands going downhill? You don't buy another in a hurry. So Chrysler bottomed out in '58, and Ford's much-touted Edsel didn't even begin to look good. However, 1958 was a recession year and everyone suffered.

Changes were few at Cadillac; its engineers and designers were feverishly putting the '59s together, no doubt measuring the tops of their fins against those of Chrysler. Of the few modifications handed out to '58 Cadillacs, the most noticeable were those to the grille and headlights.

The grille was wider and narrower, and made up of little chrome knobs. This was the first time since 1941 that Cadillac deviated from an eggcrate pattern of one form or another. The grille, which was manufactured using a new stamping process, must have been a horror to clean. Imagine polishing well over a hundred tiny, cylindrical grille extensions.

This year the fins were changed to resemble those of the Eldorado Biarritz and the Seville – keeping them in the

Above: to design and build an interior like this today would bankrupt any auto company. Facing page: teeny tail fins stand proudly aloft; note exhaust outlets in rear bumper.

Previous pages: massive bumper projections on the 1955 Cadillacs eclipsed anything that had gone before. Top: the 331-cubic-inch V8 provided able performance, winning first place in the one mile acceleration runs at the 1955 Daytona Speed Week. Above: it looked nice, but overuse of chrome caused annoying reflections in the instrument panel. Facing page: the Cadillac Fleetwood 60 Special looks every bit the New World Aristocrat. Overleaf: the second owner of this 1956 Sedan de Ville hardtop has driven this beautiful car daily since 1959, testimony of the car's superb quality. Even the paint is original.

SPECIFICATIONS
1955

Series 62 (wb 129.0)		Weight	Price	Production
6219	sdn 4d	4,370	3,977	45,300
6237	htp cpe	4,358	3,882	27,879
6237D	Coupe de Ville htp cpe	4,424	4,305	33,300
6267	conv cpe	4,627	4,448	8,150
6267S	Eldorado conv cpe	4,809	6,286	3,950
62	chassis	—	—	7
Series 60 Special (wb 133.0)				
6019	sdn 4d	4,540	4,728	18,300
Series 75 (wb 149.8)				
7523	sdn 4d, 8P	5,020	6,187	1,075
7533	limo 8P	5,113	6,402	841
8680S	comm chassis (wb 158.0)	—	—	1,975

1955 Engines	bore × stroke	bhp	availability
V8, 331.0	3.81 × 3.63	250	S-62, 60S, 75
V8, 331.0	3.81 × 3.63	270	S-Eldorado

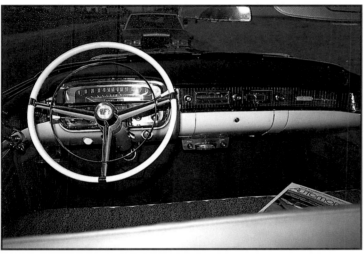

SPECIFICATIONS
1956

Series 62 (wb 129.0)		Weight	Price	Production
6219	sdn 4d	4,430	4,296	26,666
6237	htp cpe	4,420	4,201	26,649
6237D	Coupe de Ville htp cpe	4,445	4,624	24,086
6237S	Eldorado Seville htp cpe	4,665	6,556	3,900
6239D	Sedan de Ville htp cpe	4,550	4,753	41,732
6267	conv cpe	4,645	4,766	8,300
6267S	Eldorado Biarritz conv cpe	4,880	6,556	2,150
62	chassis	—	—	19
Series 60 Special (wb 133.0)				
6019	sdn 4d	4,610	5,047	17,000
Series 75 (wb 149.8)				
7523	sdn 4d, 8P	5,050	6,613	1,095
7533	limo 8P	5,130	6,828	955
8680S	comm chassis (wb 158.0)	—	—	2,025

1956 Engines	bore × stroke	bhp	availability
V8, 365.0	4.00 × 3.63	285	S-62, 60S, 75
V8, 365.0	4.00 × 3.63	305	S-Eldorado

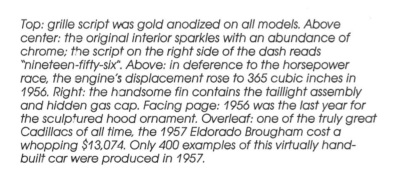

Top: grille script was gold anodized on all models. Above center: the original interior sparkles with an abundance of chrome; the script on the right side of the dash reads "nineteen-fifty-six". Above: in deference to the horsepower race, the engine's displacement rose to 365 cubic inches in 1956. Right: the handsome fin contains the taillight assembly and hidden gas cap. Facing page: 1956 was the last year for the sculptured hood ornament. Overleaf: one of the truly great Cadillacs of all time, the 1957 Eldorado Brougham cost a whopping $13,074. Only 400 examples of this virtually hand-built car were produced in 1957.

family, as it were. These had even more chrome, such as useless little strips below the taillight rocket pods, and an odd little simulated scoop ahead of the front wheel arch. Exhausts still came through the bumpers, as they had since 1954. This dubious feature was a great way to chew up rear bumpers, but one could be forgiven for thinking it looked good; after all, it did when the cars were new. Another important highlight common to all '58s was the inclusion of dual headlights. Quad headlights were passed into law by all forty-eight states and the industry switched overnight.

Horsepower still held sway, even if there were rumblings of dissent from unwelcome quarters such as insurance companies. Even though the American Manufacturers' Association had slapped a racing ban on Detroit, the message obviously fell on deaf ears at Cadillac, who boosted Eldorado's horsepower to 335. Displacement was still the whopping 365 cubic inches dished out in 1956 and was more than enough to haul this car sweetly down the road, especially if it came with triple two-barrel carburetors. Ordinary Caddies made do with 310 bhp.

Hudson had gone, Nash had gone, Packard had gone, the independents were dropping like flies. Studebaker hung in there and would get a slight reprieve, while gutsy American Motors, headed by entrepreneur George Romney, was making hay with a fast-growing clientele who wanted a small car, or at least a return to manageable size. The "bigger is better" balloon, pursued with increasing intensity by the Big Three, was about to burst in their faces, but not before some of the largest, most expensive cars of the decade had rolled out of Detroit.

From its stainless steel roof and center opening "suicide" doors to its razor-edged fins, the Brougham was an artistic tour de force. Above: the Brougham's fender outline and dual head-lights, which still had to be passed by law in most states in 1957.

Top: center-opening doors allow unhampered entry; the front seat automatically moves back when the doors are opened and returns to its preset position when doors are closed. Note the stubby door pillar, the mark of a true hardtop. Above: chromed ashtray, lighter, and a sliding door handle grace the driver's door. Facing page top: the Brougham's engine compartment appears more crowded than usual for Cadillac. Beneath the large air cleaner rests a Carter or Rochester four bbl carburetor. Facing page bottom left: the autronic eye, a $48.20 option on most Cadillacs, dips headlights for oncoming traffic. Facing page bottom right: sharp fins house delicate taillights, while below are the bullet-shaped bumper guards, and exhaust outlets.

SPECIFICATIONS
1957

Series 62 (wb 129.5)		Weight	Price	Production
6237	htp cpe	4,565	4,677	25,120
6237D	Coupe de Ville htp cpe	4,620	5,116	23,813
6237S	Eldorado Seville htp cpe	4,810	7,286	2,100
6239	htp sdn	4,595	4,781	32,342
6239D	Sedan de Ville htp cpe	4,655	5,256	23,808
6239S	Eldorado Seville htp sdn	4,810	7,286	4
6267	conv cpe	4,730	5,293	9,000
6267S	Eldorado Biarritz conv cpe	4,930	7,286	1,800
62	chassis & export sdn	—	—	385
Series 60 Special (wb 133.0)				
6039	htp sdn	4,735	5,614	24,000
Series 70 Eldorado Brougham (wb 129.0)				
7059	htp sdn	5,315	13,074	400
Series 75 (wb 149.8)				
7523	sdn 4d, 8P	5,340	7,440	1,010
7533	limo 8P	5,390	7,678	890
8680S	comm chassis (wb 156.0)	—	—	2,169

1957 Engines	bore × stroke	bhp	availability
V8, 365.0	4.00 × 3.63	300	S-62, 60S, 70
V8, 365.0	4.00 × 3.63	325	S-Eldorado

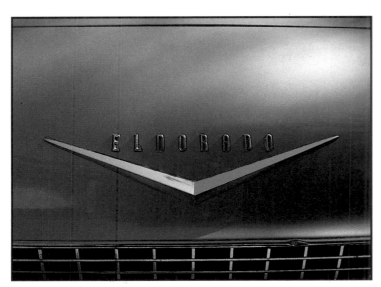

Top: the engraved plate was another little touch exclusive to the Eldorado. Above center: the Eldorado name replaced the familiar shield above the traditional "vee", the shield appearing on the front fenders. Above: six-way power seat controls; red and green arrows allowed two positions to be selected for two

"Fins ain't what they used to be," Chrysler probably lamented, stuck with less attractive, warmed-over 1959 offerings. Admittedly, their quality was better, but the company still had a long way to go if it was to assure potential customers its cars wouldn't fall apart in the first rain storm. And if Chrysler was to hum the above tune then its designers were obviously referring to the fins emerging on GM's 1959 cars.

Tall fins, flat fins, vee'd fins, even canted fins – give the GM stylists credit for imagination. Nobody could have done better. But wait! What did Cadillac have to offer?

If one is able to term cars in artists' language, then the early Fifties had to be the Baroque period – the cars then seeming soft and fleshy, like a Rubens' nude. The mid-Fifties would have been the Impressionist era, 1958 a struggle to find form and 1959 most definitely the Surrealist period. Led by Cadillac, the absolute king of the Salvador Dali school of surrealism, Cadillac's fins were so high they could scrape the top of the Sears Tower! These enormous fins began their journey just before the rear roof pillar, getting larger and higher until they almost soared out of sight! Edged in chrome and sharp enough for the Mafia to use when eliminating "problems", the fins probably served a dual purpose – to surpass Chrysler and to take Cadillac into the space age.

Sputniks, Atlas rockets, Flash Gordon and all – Cadillac was right at home with its '59 styling. If the fins weren't a strong enough message, then the studded grille, the twin nacelles at either end of the huge bumper, and the new compound, curved windshield certainly were. If you didn't get the drift, you never would!

As in 1958, the grille was made up of little chrome pods – trillions of them. A thin, chrome bar interrupted this galaxy of shining stars, but in no way did it relieve the nightmare of cleaning the grille when the dreaded day came around.

The grille theme was continued across the lower rear deck below the trunk lid. Huge, round nacelles flanked the rear bumper and housed the backup lights. Above these pseudo exhaust outlets, set in the center of the fins, twin, heavily chromed pods carried red, bullet-like projections that housed the directional signals and brake lights. Probably the stylists wished to convey the impression that these were flaring rocket exhausts upon take off.

The long slab sides were relatively free of embellishment with the exception of the Series 60 Special. This had a simulated scoop stretching the length of the rear fender, coming to a point ahead of the bumper nacelle. A fine chrome trim strip began at the front lights, wrapped itself round the dummy scoop and returned along the body side, ending just behind the front wheel arch. This was exclusive to the 60 Special, which was offered as a four-door sedan only.

In this year of excess, Cadillac also offered a flatter roof, available only on four-door, four-window models. Much longer, this roof, which succeeded in protecting rear passengers from sun stroke, was supported by ultra-thin chrome pillars covering the largest expanse of glass ever seen in an automobile. Can you imagine the cost of replacing either front or rear glass? Sadly, no manufacturer could afford to make and shape glass like this anymore.

Interiors of '59 Cadillacs were quite subdued, as even

different drivers. Facing page: "Dagmars," named after a famous TV actress whose attributes were considerable, were rubber-tipped, leaving nothing to the imagination! Styling, if a little radical, had perfect continuity, and elegant proportions.

Above: the beautiful Eldorado Brougham interior shouts quality; note the air conditioner under the dash, and the distortion free wraparound glass. Left: elegant taillights are nicely positioned in the fin and bumper, while the gas filler door is easy to find alongside the fin. Note the exhaust opening in the bumper below the fin. Facing page top: suicide doors provide good ingress, even if the huge dogleg pillar might hamper the overweight. Facing page bottom: simple dual lights integrate well with the overall design.

SPECIFICATIONS
1958

Series 62 (wb 129.5)		Weight	Price	Production
6237	htp cpe	4,630	4,784	18,736
6237D	Coupe de Ville htp cpe	4,705	5,251	18,414
6237S	Eldorado Seville htp cpe	4,910	7,500	855
6239	htp sdn	4,675	4,891	13,335
6239E	htp sdn (ext. deck)	4,770	5,079	20,952
6239	Sedan de Ville htp sdn	4,855	5,497	23,989
6267	conv cpe	4,856	5,454	7,825
6267S	Eldorado Biarritz conv cpe	5,070	7,500	815
62	chassis & exp sdn	—	—	206
Series 60 Special (wb 133.0)				
6039	htp sdn	4,930	6,232	12,900
Series 70 Eldorado Brougham (wb 126.0)				
7059	htp sdn	5,315	13,074	304
Series 75 (wb 149.8)				
7523	sdn 4d, 8P	5,360	8,460	802
7533	limo 8P	5,425	8,675	730
8680S	comm chassis (wb 156.0)	—	—	1,915

1958 Engine	bore × stroke	bhp	availability
V8, 365.0	4.00 × 3.63	310	S-all

69

SPECIFICATIONS
1959

Series 62 (wb 130.0)		Weight	Price	Production
6229	htp sdn 6W	4,770	5,080	23,461
6237	htp cpe	4,690	4,892	21,947
6239	htp sdn 9W	4,835	5,080	14,138
6267	conv cpe	4,855	5,455	11,130
62	export sdn	—	—	60
De Ville (wb 130.0)				
6329	htp sdn 6W	4,850	5,498	19,158
6337	htp cpe	4,720	5,252	21,924
6339	htp sdn 4W	4,825	5,498	12,308
Eldorado (wb 130.0)				
6437	Seville htp cpe	—	7,401	975
6467	Biarritz conv cpe	—	7,401	1,320
6929	Brougham htp sdn	—	13,075	99
Series 60 Special (wb 133.0)				
6039	htp sdn	4,890	6,233	12,250
Series 75 (wb 149.8)				
6723	sdn 4d, 9P	5,490	9,533	710
6733	limo 9P	5,570	9,748	690
6890	comm chassis (wb 156.0)	—	—	2,102

1959 Engines	bore × stroke	bhp	availability
V8, 390.0	4.00 × 3.88	325	S-62, DeVille, 60S, 75
V8, 390.0	4.00 × 3.88	345	S-Eldorado

the two-tone leather-and-cloth combination used attractive hues. Instruments were set into an easy-to-read panel and, though the size and shape of the '59s didn't inspire confidence, the actual handling and ride were considerable improvements on previous years.

Both the Eldorado Biarritz and the Seville returned and were recognizable by their own special chrome trim. Even after the demise of the fabulous Brougham, Cadillac resurrected the name for a special Eldorado built at Pininfarina's body shop in Turin. Its styling was more formal, the fins actually modest. Cadillac would send the chassis to Italy, the body was installed and then the completed cars would come back to Detroit for finishing. Ninety-nine Eldos were built this way in 1959, making this model a rare collector's item today.

Once again Cadillac raised its horsepower: 325 for standard models and 345 for all the Eldorados, boring its flexible V8 to 390 cubic inches. In ten years, horsepower had more than doubled, yet performance was only marginally improved, and this was destined to be the last year before 1964 that horsepower ratings would alter.

1959 was the year that Buddy Holly, "Big Bopper" and Richie Valens died when their plane crashed on the way to a show. Elvis was in the army, Frank Lloyd Wright died and Fidel Castro ousted the Mafia and took over Cuba. In Detroit at the end of that year a trio of entirely different cars rolled out of Detroit: the Falcon, Corvair and Valiant. Small, and tastefully designed, the compacts were the opposite of 1959s motoring excesses. How Cadillac would fare in a down-sized world was going to be interesting.

Chrysler gave the world fins in '57, but Cadillac's were the biggest in '59. Outrageous styling belonging to the Salvador Dali surrealist school brought the Fifties to a close.

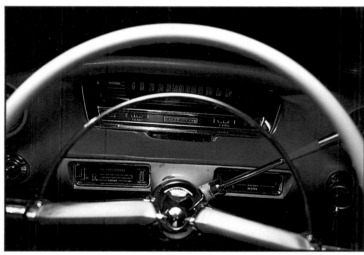

Top: razor-sharp fins, rocket exhaust taillights and huge nacelle suggested outer space and John Glenn. In contrast, the instrument panel (above) was clean and simple in design. Right: its flamboyance apart, the 1959 Eldorado Seville had a lot going for it, including surprisingly good handling. The engine had grown to 390 cubic inches.

1960-1969

Even though most motoring scribes hated the 1959 Cadillac's styling, the general public obviously didn't share their aversion if the sale of over 142,000 units was anything to go by. Nevertheless, Cadillac's designers obviously weren't sure whether they had done the right thing and set about rectifying the car for 1960. What they did deserves a great deal of credit: they took the flamboyance and vulgarity out of Cadillac, turning it instead into a conservative, well-proportioned vehicle more in keeping with what people had come to expect of America's foremost luxury car.

Spaced with fine horizontal bars, Cadillac's 1960 full-width grille still relied on rows of cheerful little chrome studs in between. Somebody at Cadillac must have hated people who polish their cars, for while the new grille was pleasing to the eye, it was next to impossible to clean. There was no center bar that year, but the bumper was less outrageous than before.

Good taste had returned and one look at the rear told why. Somebody had decapitated the fins, bringing them down to sensible levels – 1959's conversation piece had been chopped. Though only an inch had actually been carved off them, styling created the illusion that they were much lower, while the rocket-flame taillights and huge bumper nacelles were replaced by oval units set vertically and containing most of the rear lights. Supplementing these was a slim taillight blended into the end of the fin.

For the first time in years, Cadillac did not have a futuristic showcar to display at GM's lavish Motoramas. Probably the 1959 Batmobile – the glass-bubbled, ultra-finned XP-74 Cyclone – was as far as the stylists could legitimately go without bringing the guffaws of a nation down round their heads. It was an absurd car with little to recommend it, unlike the sporty LeMans of 1952, or the 1954 El Camino and Park Avenue of 1954. Showcars were styling exercises often predicting design elements that would show up on future production-line Cadillacs. Historians should compare the 1954 Park Avenue with British GM's 1957 Vauxhall; the resemblance is extraordinary!

1960 came to a close and Cadillac sales had moved up 2,000 units over 1959, which is one way of saying the country was split over the controversial '59 styling. In their first year, the new compacts sold briskly and there would be a bunch more in 1961. John F. Kennedy became President by a paper-thin majority and the world awaited whatever 1961 would bring.

Different Cadillacs, that's for sure.

Whether the fashion for shorter cars had anything to do with Cadillac's back-pedalling on size is anybody's guess. Lincoln came out with a beautiful new Continental that was fifteen inches shorter than the dinosaur 1958-60 models and had quality no other U.S. automaker could match, including Cadillac. So Cadillac contented itself with a total restyle, which was crisp and yet featured a good deal of metal sculpturing, while slashing its overall length by some three inches.

Lower tailfins, a flatter hoodline, flush-fitting fenders cut away round the large, chromed dual headlight bezels and another version of the polisher's purgatory, the studded grille, highlighted Cadillac's new look. In keeping with the more conservative styling was the all-new windshield –

Cadillac described its new 1960 models as "... more inspiring to behold ..." and, considering the wild extremes of 1959, it was a fair description.

SPECIFICATIONS
1960

Series 62 (wb 130.0)		Weight	Price	Production
6229	htp sdn 6W	4,805	5,080	26,824
6237	htp cpe	4,670	4,892	19,978
6239	htp sdn 4W	4,775	5,080	9,984
6267	conv cpe	4,850	5,455	14,000
62	chassis & export sdn	—	—	38
De Ville (wb 130.0)				
6329	htp sdn 6W	4,835	5,498	22,579
6337	htp cpe	4,705	5,252	21,585
6339	htp sdn 4W	4,815	5,498	9,225
Eldorado (wb 130.0)				
6437	Seville htp cpe	—	7,401	1,075
6467	Biarritz conv cpe	—	7,401	1,285
6929	Brougham htp sdn	—	13,075	101
Series 60 Special (wb 130.0)				
6039	htp sdn	4,880	6,233	11,800
Series 75 (wb 149.8)				
6723	sdn 4d, 9P	5,475	9,533	718
6733	limo 9P	5,560	9,748	832
6890	comm chassis (wb 156.0)	—	—	2,160

1960 Engines	bore × stroke	bhp	availability
V8, 390.0	4.00 × 3.88	325	S-62, DeVille, 60S, 75
V8, 390.0	4.00 × 3.88	345	S-Eldorado

gone was the familiar dogleg, to be replaced by flat, sloping glass supported by steeply raked windshield pillars that tucked under where the fender met the door.

A flat roof, sculptured body lines, oval, horizontally-placed taillights and a lower, chrome-edged body skeg molding made up Cadillac's new look. It is hard to say whether it improved upon 1960's redesign – a large body of people didn't think it did. You can never please everybody, and if you hold an elevated position like Cadillac does, it's natural for there to be detractors; it's one of the penalties of being famous.

Cadillac's 1961 model year production totalled 138,379, almost 4,000 units fewer than the previous year. Cadillac would not have worried, though: the new, much-praised Lincoln Continental only produced 26,164 units, while Chrysler's Imperial only managed a desultory 12,058.

One mechanical item which quietly disappeared in 1961 was air suspension. Most American car makers tried it following its successful use in the revolutionary Citroen DS19 in 1955, but no American air suspension system worked, least of all the system used by GM. It had been offered on Cadillacs of one form or another since 1957, starting with

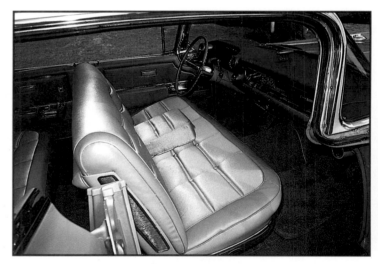

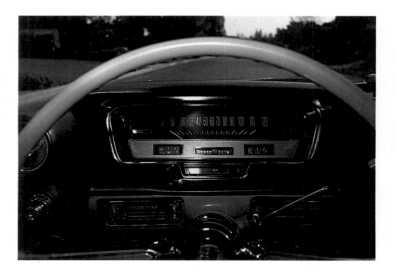

From its elegant roofline and its crisp, unadorned sides to its lowered fins, the 1960 Cadillac (these and previous pages) won praise for its quiet, restrained good taste. Top right: compound curved glass like this would cost a fortune today. Center right: like the exterior, the 1960 Cadillac interior was noticeable for its absence of glitz. Right: the instrument panel was little changed from 1959.

SPECIFICATIONS
1961

Series 62 (wb 129.5)		Weight	Price	Production
6229	htp sdn 6W	4,680	5,080	26,216
6237	htp cpe	4,560	4,892	16,005
6239	htp sdn 4W	4,660	5,080	4,700
6267	conv	4,720	5,455	15,500
62	chassis	—	—	5
De Ville (wb 129.5)				
6239	htp sdn 6W	4,710	5,498	26,415
6337	htp cpe	4,595	5,252	20,156
6339	htp sdn 4W	4,715	5,498	4,847
6399	Town Sedan htp 6W	—	5,498	3,756
Eldorado (wb 129.5)				
6367	Biarritz conv cpe	—	6,477	1,450
Series 60 Special (wb 129.5)				
6039	htp sdn	4,770	6,233	15,500
Series 75 (wb 149.8)				
6723	sdn 4d, 9P	5,390	9,533	600
6733	limo 9P	5,420	9,748	926
6890	comm chassis (wb 156.0)	—	—	2,204

1961 Engine	bore × stroke	bhp	availability
V8, 390.0	4.00 × 3.88	325	S-all

A new windshield design and sculptured flanks highlighted the 1961 Cadillacs, note the lower, canted fin, which added to the new, sharper look. Above: dual lights nestle under the flat hood and fender line.

1961 CADILLAC SERIES 62 CONVERTIBLE

the Eldorado Brougham. The suspension on most Broughams collapsed and owners reverted to a coil-spring conversion instead. Yet Cadillac continued to offer the same system on other models until 1960, when they finally got the message that this system wasn't going to work. It is fortunate that air suspension was only an option on standard Cadillacs.

1962 was Cadillac's sixtieth anniversary and, although styling changes were few, the first new sales record in six years was chalked up – a massive model year production figure of 160,840. Although all other makes increased production too, not least Lincoln and Imperial who went up over 30,000 and 14,000 respectively, nobody could catch Cadillac. Its standing as America's luxury sales leader was unassailable. Or so it seemed at the time.

New, wider rear roof pillars adorned five of Cadillac's thirteen models. More formal, they added distinction and were a sign of things to come. Many would heave a sigh of relief at the sight of the squared, formal shape Cadillac was evolving – perhaps 1959 was only a bad dream, after all.

The most noteworthy technical advance was the implementation of a new dual safety braking system. Independent pistons and brake fluid reservoirs were provided for front and rear brakes, assuring that at least one set would work should the other fail. This system was standard throughout the line.

If 1962 was a record year for Cadillac, 1963 was going to be even better. For a start, Cadillac was all new and more formal, more like a person's idea of how a Cadillac should be. Even the engine received attention for the first time in fifteen years.

Body lines for 1963 were what one might call razor-edged, even angular – except at the front end, which bore more than a passing resemblance to the 1959 Cadillac. The grille, though a crosshatch design, was split in two by a center bar and had Cadillac script in the lower left-hand corner. For the first time since 1960, Cadillac returned to a chamfered hood flanked by fenders with rounded "brows" over the dual lights. Below these were small parking lights set into grille extensions rather than into the simple, redesigned bumper.

Once again the fins were lower and the taillights stacked into vertical, oval-shaped pods, which had a tendency to de-emphasize the fins even further. As for the windshield, it was the best-looking one Cadillac had for years; raked at a steep angle, there wasn't a trace of dogleg anywhere – just slim, straight pillars.

Inside, the interiors were luxurious in typical Cadillac fashion, but much more restrained. They were roomier than 1962, though only an inch was added to the overall length. There were five series comprising twelve models, one less than in 1962. All, except the Fleetwood 75s, shared the X member chassis and while that was much the same as before, the engine had a shorter and narrower cast-iron cylinder block and alloy timing gear. These, plus many new internal components, were lighter, thus reducing engine weight by fifty pounds. Bore and stroke, horsepower and displacement carried on from before.

It was a great year for Cadillac, and an even greater one for GM Chief Stylist, William Mitchell, whose magnificent new Corvette Stingray and Buick Riviera drew rave reviews and had the motor industry standing on its head. Another wonderful GM car was Pontiac's Grand Prix, undeniably one of the prettiest cars on the road. 1963 was the year of four entirely distinctive cars – GM had never had it so good and wouldn't do so again.

Three Series 62 models, four Series 63, one Series 60, one

Top: the fins show up well here, although the large oval looks a little awkward. Above: it's hard to believe, but the '61 Cadillac's width was a massive 6 feet 7¾ inches. Facing page top: the beautiful hubcap shows the lengths designers went to to create a wealth of detail. Facing page bottom: Cadillac's obsession with little chrome pods entered its final year – by 1962 they were gone, and numerous weekend polishers heaved a sigh of relief!

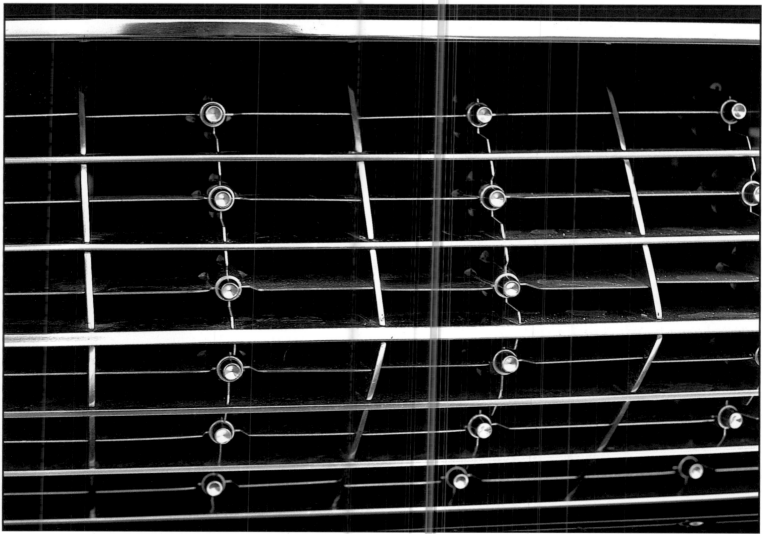

1964 CADILLAC SERIES 62 COUPE DE VILLE

Eldorado (now the Fleetwood Eldorado) and two Series 75 cars were announced for 1964, totalling eleven models in all. As in previous years, the 129.5-inch wheelbase served all models except the exclusive 75s, which used the 149.7-inch wheelbase.

Changes to the cars were modest, there being a few slight modifications to the grille and the rear. The one big change was under the hood: the engine's displacement was raised to 429 cubic inches and the horsepower to 340. Also new was the Turbo Hydra-Matic torque converter transmission which was standard on all models. As far as displacement went, there was no larger engine than Cadillac's, even if Chrysler outdid them on horsepower (390 vs. 340).

Cadillac boasted its 500,000th air-conditioned car sale, noting that seventy-five percent of its output had this by 1964, at $474 extra – small beer for the additional comfort air-conditioning brings. That meant approximately 133,000 Cadillacs, from a total 165,959 Cadillacs built in 1964, had air conditioning.

All new, re-engineered and redesigned – that was Cadillac for 1965, and so extensive were these changes that Cadillac's promotional literature boasted it was the most thorough model change in the company's history.

With the exception of the Series 75, all Cadillacs had a new box-section perimeter frame, which was claimed to have more torsional rigidity, coupled with better ride and handling characteristics. It was also claimed to be one of the quietest Cadillacs on record, with the smoothness of its operations unequaled by any other make. An option on most, but standard on the Fleetwood 60 Special and Eldorado, was the provision of automatic self-levelling suspension, which maintained the car at a constant level, regardless of weight in the trunk or passenger compartment.

Completely restyled, the new Cadillacs were crisper and more severe than ever. Unlike the bump-and-bulge designs of six years earlier, those of 1965 were noticeable for their simplicity. Apart from a fine rubbing strip along the center, the bevelled body lines flowed cleanly from stem to stern, ending in vertically-positioned chrome bumper nacelles housing the rear lights.

What? No fins? That's right. They had been getting lower each year since their peak in 1959, and now the famous fins – perhaps Cadillac's most distinguishing feature since 1948 – had finally gone.

At the front, a new cross-hatched grille was flanked by vertically stacked dual headlights protruding ahead of the hood. Directly beneath the lights, the new front bumper was massive, yet it afforded little or no protection for the protruding fenders.

Variable-ratio power steering was standard on all 1966 Cadillacs, and either standard or an option on all other GM cars. With variable ratio, the effort required to steer changes depending on the car's speed; if the car is traveling fast the effort required to steer is greater than if the car is being parked or driven slowly, when it became much lighter. Exterior changes were minor, the removal of the parking lights from the bumper to the grille being the only noticeable difference.

So far, little mention has been made of the stately

Crisp, clean styling set off this 1964 Series 62 model. Fins were still to be seen, but they had become an endangered species! The 390-cubic-inch V8 put out 340 bhp.

1964 CADILLAC SERIES 62 COUPE DE VILLE

Fleetwood 75 Series. This series had not had a completely new body since 1959, so in 1966 the model that was probably used to chauffeur more of the rich and famous than any other was finally updated, getting the box section perimeter frame and the 1966 styling that lent itself so well to the lengthy limousines.

Ford's Thunderbird pioneered the regular production line luxury personal car – that is, a car with two doors and individual styling unlike that of other models. Pontiac's Grand Prix was a personal car, so too was the Buick Riviera; even Chevy and Chrysler came out later on with the Monte Carlo and Cordoba. Then in 1966 Oldsmobile outdid them all with their fabulous, highly styled, front-wheel-drive Toronado. A year later Cadillac launched its stunning front-wheel-drive Fleetwood Eldorado Coupe.

Based on GM's "E" body shell shared with Toronado and Riviera, the new Eldorado was built on its own assembly line. Its wheelbase was 120 inches long and its overall length 221 inches, some six-and-a-half inches shorter than Cadillac's Series 60 Special. Its styling was almost Teutonic and quite different from its "E"-body cousins. There was no similarity between any of the three models, a point worth remembering for future reference.

The design followed the long hood, short deck theme popularized by Thunderbird, Mustang and the Riviera. Over fifty-three inches high, the Eldorado had a definite sporting flair, boasting full wheel openings, natty wheel covers and an exclusive "V"-shaped rear window. At the front was Cadillac's familiar crosshatch grille, but this one had a pronounced "V" point at the center. Behind the grille were

SPECIFICATIONS
1964

Series 62 (wb 129.5)		Weight	Price	Production
6229	htp sdn 6W	4,575	5,236	9,243
6239	htp sdn 4W	4,550	5,236	13,670
6257	htp cpe	4,475	5,048	12,166
6267	conv cpe	4,545	5,612	17,900
De Ville (wb 129.5)				
6329	htp sdn 6W	4,600	5,655	14,627
6339	htp sdn 4W	4,575	5,655	39,674
6357	htp cpe	4,495	5,408	38,195
Eldorado (wb 129.5)				
6367	Biarritz conv cpe	4,605	6,630	1,870
Series 60 Special (wb 129.5)				
6039	htp sdn	4,680	6,388	14,550
Series 75 (wb 149.8)				
6723	sdn 4d, 9P	5,215	9,746	617
6733	limo 9P	5,300	9,960	808
6890	comm chassis (wb 156.0)	—	—	2,639

1964 Engine	bore × stroke	bhp	availability
V8, 429.0	4.13 × 4.00	340	S-all

A colossal grille tells the world this is a Cadillac. Grilles generally may have changed over the years, but Cadillac followed an evolutionary course rather than going for radical change.

dual headlights hidden by covers that dropped out of sight when the lights came on. Under the hood was the same 429-cubic-inch, 340-horse V8 as in other Cadillacs, more than enough to propel the Eldorado along at considerable speed.

Due to its front-wheel-drive design, the Eldorado was markedly different from anything else on the road – the exception, of course, being its cousin the Toronado. For instance the Turbo Hydra-Matic was positioned to the left of the engine. Power was transferred from the converter through the transmission gear sets to a differential at the front of the transmission, which was split between the front wheels. No tensioners were used on the Hy-Vo driving chain which did the power transference, as all the chains ran on devices that pre-stretched them.

The front suspension consisted of A-arms set at the upper and lower levels, torsion bars and anti-roll bars. At the rear the drop center live axle had parallel, single-leaf springs as well as four shocks mounted vertically and horizontally. All told, the ride was good and the handling excellent for a car of this type.

It goes without saying that the Eldorado eclipsed the other Cadillac models in 1967, though the standard Cadillacs were helped at this time by a modest facelift. A crease line had been added to their fenders, starting at the front and becoming more apparent at the rear, where quite a pronounced waistline dip began just forward of the roof pillar. At the front, the newly designed crosshatch grille leaned forward, following the contours of the front fenders.

The mid to late Sixties belonged to the Rolling Stones, Timothy Leary, Flower Power – and the mighty muscle cars. It was at this time that Ralph Nader was making a name for himself in his crusade against the auto industry's poor safety standards. His attention focused on the Corvair, and

in a typical David and Goliath scenario Ralph Nader won his case against the car and the industry, which was forced to clean up its act by the government. So, in 1967 the first safety features began to appear. Like other car makers, Cadillac shovelled in extra dash padding, included a breakaway interior mirror and recessed knobs and, most important of all, added an energy-absorbing steering column designed to save the driver from severe injury in event of an accident.

After several years using just two wheelbases, 1967 saw Cadillac's offering jump to four. The Calais was given 129.5 inches, then the Sixty Special and the Brougham went to 133 inches. Already mentioned was the Eldorado's 120 inches, while the Seventy-Five models stayed with 149.8 inches. This diversity of product didn't appear to do any harm; Cadillac realized its dream and produced 200,000 cars for the first time in 1967, exceeding this magnificent total by 30,003 units a year later.

As was usual with second year models, Cadillac's 1968 crop came out with modest styling revisions. Most of the modifications were at the front, including the hood, which was lengthened by six-and-a half inches to the base of the windshield. This enabled Cadillac to try out hidden windshield wipers, concealing them below the upward turned rear hoodline. It was a styling gimmick that has stayed for twenty-one years and the way things look, it will

Above: smaller fins crown the bumper extensions, which house backup and parking lights. Facing page top: the rear deck looks big enough to land a helicopter on! Facing page bottom: the restrained interior of the '64 Coupe de Ville is both functional and good looking.

SPECIFICATIONS 1967

Calais (wb 129.5)		Weight	Price	Production
68247	htp cpe	4,447	5,040	9,085
68249	htp sdn	4,495	5,215	9,880
68269	sdn 4d	4,499	5,215	2,865
De Ville (wb 129.5)				
68347	htp cpe	4,486	5,392	52,905
68349	htp sdn	4,532	5,625	59,902
68367	conv cpe	4,479	5,608	18,202
68369	sdn 4d	4,534	5,625	8,800
Eldorado (wb 120.0)				
69347	htp cpe	4,500	6,277	17,930
Sixty Special (wb 133.0)				
68069	sdn 4d	4,678	6,423	3,550
68169	Fleetwood Brougham sdn 4d	4,715	6,739	12,750
Seventy-Five (wb 149.8)				
69723	sdn 4d, 9P	5,344	10,360	835
69733	limo 9P	5,436	10,571	965
68490	comm chassis (wb 156.0)	—	—	2,333

1967 Engine	bore × stroke	bhp	availability
V8, 429.0	4.13 × 4.00	340	S-all

Most of Cadillac's hype centered round the new Eldorado, but the 1967 Fleetwood (these and previous pages) remained luxury king. Actually, fewer Fleetwoods were made than Eldorados: 12,850 versus 17,930. Facing page: an American dream come true: the 1967 Cadillac Fleetwood Brougham.

still be there in a further twenty-one years. Like other Cadillacs, Eldorado added inches to its hood – four-and-a-half inches to be exact. This allowed for the provision of hidden wipers, thus enhancing the car's already-beautiful lines. New parking lights and turning signals were built into the leading edges of the front fenders, while the side marker lights were cleverly disguised with Cadillac's traditional wreath.

Hardly a year goes by without Cadillac doing something of note. 1968 it was another all-new engine. Standard in all models, the 472-cubic-inch engine was the largest production-car engine in the world. Horsepower, at 375, was modest by comparison, while the compression ratio was 10.25:1.

Why a new engine so soon after the redesign in 1963? Well, it was true that the engineers could go no further with what was essentially a nineteen-year-old design. Yet there was also need for an engine with fewer parts for ease of maintenance, and for lower production-line costs – plus a requirement for one that could be tailored to the soon-to-be applied emissions standards. This engine was the first in the industry to have air-conditioning compressor mounts already built in – evidently something important to the client, as ninety-six percent of all Cadillac buyers demanded air conditioning.

On June 19, 1969 Cadillac built its 4-millionth car, but the year's total was down to 223,237. This was nothing when one considers the three million cars built since 1949, and the forty-seven years it took to build the first million. Although it is doubtful that the quality was the same as in those cars of the first forty-seven years, it was a magnificent achievement just the same.

Revisions to Cadillac's front for 1969 were quite extensive. 1968's vertical headlamps were replaced by horizontal dual units either side of the very central, crosshatched grille, while parking lamps and turn signals wrapped around the front fenders. The body sides were much as before, but separate taillights were positioned vertically in the rear fenders.

Eleven models on four wheelbases were the same as 1968. There were four DeVille models, including Cadillac's one and only convertible, two Calais models and five Fleetwoods, including the 75s, Eldorado and 60 Special.

Eldorado lost its concealed headlamps for exposed ones in 1969 and didn't look quite as refined as a result. A new padded vinyl roof was available, but as more features became standard on all Cadillacs, the options list grew smaller with each successive year. Thankfully, the heater had become standard by this time, though the AM radio was still an option. And so on a warmer, though more silent note, the decade for Cadillac drew to a close.

Facing page top: the 1967 Cadillac interior featured attractive brocades and bags of room. Facing page bottom: if your car carried this time-honored name then you had truly arrived – the key to the executive restroom was yours! Overleaf: this rather overdone 1970 Fleetwood limousine used to belong to one-time country and western singer Johnny Paycheck, whose hit Take Your Job and Shove It became the factory worker's anthem.

1970-1989

Enter 1970 and a new decade – one that saw a complete turnabout in people's buying habits and a beleaguered motor industry with its back to the wall. By the mid-Eighties the American automobile had changed almost beyond recognition – to trot out phrases like "big is better" or "there's no substitute for cubes" in motordom's hallowed halls would be tantamount to treachery.

Apart from the rumbling of disgruntled insurance companies and even stiffer Federal legislation concerning safety and emissions, Detroit greeted 1970 with few worries on its plate. Over at Cadillac the joint was jumping with the debut of a massive 500-cubic-inch (8.2-litre), 400-horsepower engine. This colossus was intended for the Eldorado only, but eventually found its way under the hoods of all Cadillacs by 1976. There was nothing innovative about this engine, apart from the fact that this was the first time such a large power plant was offered as standard in a production car. Why Cadillac would bother with it when the cry was for less power, not more, may have confounded a few observers, but hindsight offers one explanation. This was to do with the sharp Lincoln Continental Mark III. Since its introduction in late 1968, it had been nipping remorselessly around Eldorado's proverbial heels. With production for the two cars running virtually neck and neck, and with no new styling in the works until 1971, Cadillac probably thought the massive engine would be a suitable stop-gap. It obviously was, as Cadillac extended the Eldorado's lead by almost 7,500 units in 1970.

Only minor details, such as a revised grille and new emblems, distinguished the rest of Cadillac's 1970 lineup Mechanically, the cars were unchanged and continued to use the 472-cubic-inch engine across the board.

Though observers might not have thought so, 1971 Cadillacs were totally redesigned. That's the beauty of Cadillac; its progression is one of continuity, rather than radical change. The changes included a marginally longer wheelbase. For the Calais and DeVille models this meant an extra half inch, bringing the wheelbase to 130 inches, while the Eldorado went up to 126.3 inches from 120. The Fleetwood Seventy-Five's already-substantial length was increased by 1.7 inches, bringing the wheelbase to 151.3 inches. Overall lengths only went up around half an inch on any model except the Fleetwood 75 Series, which was increased by two inches to a dinosaurian 247.3 inches.

Although Cadillac referred to its new lines as "tubular," due to the design's more rounded curves, they were not as attractive as those of previous years. As for the Eldorado, once crisp and sleek of line, in its new guise it had become overweight and flabby in appearance. Whether intentional or not, the rear quarter panels ballooned, thus bringing to mind the 1953 Eldorado.

Production was down to 188,537 cars in 1971 due to a three-month strike, the longest GM could recall, but nine models in three series announced Cadillac's seventieth birthday, and the company celebrated by building a record 267,787 cars. One of those cars went to Russia, a present from President Richard Nixon to Secretary Leonid Brezhnev, an admitted car enthusiast.

On June 23, 1973, Cadillac built its five-millionth car and

There are many custom coachbuilders making a profitable living remodeling Cadillacs, Lincolns, and Mercedes to the customer's choice. The mounted hood ornament (right) is not standard and nor is the vinyl-covered continental tire kit (facing page top). Facing page bottom: velour curtains, color TV and a record player announce a star is in town.

SPECIFICATIONS 1970			
Calais (wb 129.5)	**Weight**	**Price**	**Production**
68247 htp cpe	4,620	5,637	4,724
68249 htp sdn	4,680	5,813	5,187
De Ville (wb 129.5)			
68347 htp cpe	4,650	5,884	76,043
68349 htp sdn	4,725	6,118	83,274
68367 conv cpe	4,660	6,068	15,172
68369 sdn 4d	4,690	6,118	7,230
Eldorado (wb 120.0)			
69347 htp cpe	4,630	6,903	28,842
Sixty Special (wb 133.0)			
68089 sdn 4d	4,830	6,953	1,738
68189 Fleetwood Brougham sdn 4d	4,835	7,284	16,913
Seventy-Five (wb 149.8)			
69723 sdn 4d, 9P	5,530	11,039	876
69733 limo 9P	5,630	11,178	1,240
69890 comm chassis (wb 156.0)	—	—	2,506

1970 Engines	bore × stroke	bhp	availability
V8, 472.0	4.30 × 4.06	375	S-all exc Eldorado
V8, 500.0	4.30 × 4.30	400	S-Eldorado

produced a model year total of 304,839 besides, but this was hardly surprising considering 1973 was a record year for the auto industry as a whole. Ironically, buoyed by its success, the industry forecast that 1974 would be even better. Meanwhile, new chrome wheel covers, a wider grille, a revised hood and other knick-knacks identified Cadillac's standard cars. All had a new, impact-absorbing bumper which cushioned against damage in bumps of up to five miles per hour. The same system was adopted for the Eldorado, which also sported a new eggcrate-style grille.

Overbodied and overdone, the 1973 Eldorado sported more fake wood in its interior than a Holiday Inn lobby! It was done in extremely bad taste, with its whirls and twirls supposedly reminding the buyer of the days when wood carving was an art. All Cadillac succeeded in doing was to make an ugly car even uglier. Perhaps that's why Lincoln's Continental Mark IV had outsold the Eldorado and would continue to do so over the next few years.

If the industry had hoped to repeat 1973's sales figures, that hope was dashed when the Arabs shut off the oil late in 1973.

Small, fuel-efficient cars suddenly came into vogue when the gas crunch hit. Nobody wanted big cars anymore. Horrid, gas-guzzling monsters the people said, though they rushed to buy them once they learned there wouldn't be a gas shortage after all. Nevertheless, the scare was enough to encourage the industry to look at smaller cars; with sales of imported vehicles, especially those from Japan, increasing year after year, something would have to be done. Even Cadillac got into the small-car act. While its 1974 cars were moderate revisions of its existing lines, a down-sized Cadillac was close at hand.

New eggcrate grilles were bolder, more pronounced, than the fine mesh-type grille used on the Eldorado, which had restyled rear fenders that were flatter and crisper than before. All Cadillacs had grown in length, and the Eldorado grew another 8.7 inches to 230.7 inches overall. The Fleetwood Sixty Special was given what was called the "Talisman" package. Critics referred to it as obscene and decadent and it was every bit of both. With its Medici crushed velvet upholstery and reclining seats, this Cadillac could have been referred to as the travelling bordello....

Four rectangular headlights, a new grille, fixed quarter windows in the rear roof sail panels, the adoption of Eldorado's big 8.2-litre engine in all Cadillacs and new luxury options, including a power-operated glass roof panel – this was the standard Cadillac story in 1975. Another new feature was GM's high energy electronic fuel injection. Standard on the Seville, the Bendix unit was optional on all other Cadillacs. As for the Eldorado, it got full wheel openings, which it hadn't seen since 1970, while its grille was bolder and more eggcrate in design than in 1974.

And then there was the Seville. Shorter than the standard Cadillac by some twenty-seven inches, the Seville was Cadillac's answer to the European luxury car invasion which, along with Lincoln, had eroded Cadillac's base. Back in 1968, Cadillac claimed seventy-two percent of the market, but Americans discovered that there were European cars such as Mercedes, BMW and Jaguar that might conceivably be better than those from America's luxury leader. They

Right: a bird's eye view of the Fleetwood limousine, showing the unusual and somewhat ostentatious chrome-edged vinyl roof treatment. Head-turning appearance is what many Cadillac customers wanted, especially if they entrusted their car to a coachbuilder.

bought them, liked them and by 1975, Cadillac's market share had dropped to sixty-two percent – hence the Seville.

Mercedes' sales were picking up in America at quite a rate when Cadillac, at the height of the muscle car boom, decided it might be worth looking into the idea of a Mercedes-sized car. Surveys in 1970 seemed to suggest that the market would be receptive to such a model, so work was begun to build a car that would compete favorably with the illustrious German aristocrat.

Some say Cadillac came close with the Seville; some say it didn't. Considering cost limitations (just $100 million was spent on tooling) Cadillac's engineers were unable to do what they knew needed to be done. Probably another couple of hundred million dollars might have given Cadillac a world-class automobile, but GM wouldn't spend money if there was a parts bin from which a model could be cobbled. Profits, not progress, was the name of the U.S. automakers' game in the mid-Seventies.

GM's "X" body platform (Chevrolet Nova, Pontiac Ventura, Oldsmobile Omega and Buick Apollo) was extensively modified to become the Seville's "K" platform. Numerous components used on the Seville were not interchangeable with any of the aforementioned "X" cars, while an entirely different, quite attractive, body was unique for the "baby" Cadillac.

Suspension was fairly conventional, with front A-arms and coils, a live rear axle and leaf springs. Sounds rather basic, even crude, doesn't it? It was. Yet Cadillac's engineers dressed it up with special Delco Pliacell gas chamber shock absorbers, self-levelling as standard, a rear anti-roll

SPECIFICATIONS
1972

Calais (wb 130.0)		Weight	Price	Production
68247	htp cpe	4,642	5,771	3,900
68249	htp sdn	4,698	5,938	3,875
De Ville (wb 130.0)				
68347	htp cpe	4,682	6,168	95,280
68349	htp sdn	4,762	6,390	99,531
Eldorado (wb 126.3)				
69347	htp cpe	4,682	7,230	32,099
69367	conv	4,772	7,546	7,975
Sixty Special Brougham (wb 133.0)				
68169	Fleetwood sdn 4d	4,858	7,637	20,750
Seventy-Five (wb 151.5)				
69723	sdn 4d	5,515	11,748	955
69733	limo 9P	5,637	11,880	960
69890	comm chassis (wb 157.5)	—	—	2,462

1972 Engines	bore × stroke	bhp	availability
V8, 472.0	4.30 × 4.06	220	S-all exc Eldorado
V8, 500.0	4.30 × 4.30	235	S-Eldorado

In 1970 Cadillac announced to the world a new engine. Standard in the Eldorado, the 500-cubic-inch engine was the largest production engine ever to be fitted to an automobile. Following the European fad current at the time, Cadillac had "8.2 liters" positioned on the front fenders. Shown right is a pristine 1972 Eldorado fitted with this monster engine.

bar, responsive Euro-style steering and big radials mounted on fifteen-inch wheels. No extra cash was spent on brakes, so Cadillac settled for a system of front discs and rear drums.

In some respects, the Seville was Cadillac's undoing. You see, the engine was not Cadillac, it was Oldsmobile's 350-cubic-inch, 180-bhp V8. New buyers balked at having to pay $12,500 for a car that used Chevrolet parts and an Oldsmobile engine, especially as the most expensive Olds was half the Seville's price, and the Chevy even less. Still, the Seville did come with more options as standard equipment than any other Cadillac model.

Eight inches narrower and 204 inches long, the Seville's styling was restrained, to say the least. Its squared-off, straight body lines tried to make the car look European without losing sight of its American heritage, and this it did grandly. Even though many were doubtful about the price, the Seville sold well, with 16,355 built in a truncated model year that had begun in March, 1975. Meanwhile, after twelve years in production, Cadillac's low-price Calais bit the dust. Only 6,200 were built in 1976, out of a total Cadillac production figure of 309,139 – a new record.

By 1976, most American cars were filled with almost every safety feature known to the Federal authorities, and then some. Stifling emissions controls, though necessary, meant American cars had as much zip as a tortoise about to hibernate – a nightmare eventually rectified by dedicated engineers – and because the "Feds" frowned on them, the days of the romantic convertible were numbered. Or so everybody thought, including Cadillac.

Convertibles had always been part of the Cadillac mystique, the ultimate way to travel. Ever since 1916 Cadillac had been building convertibles and, while sales were never those of hardtops and coupes, they were, nevertheless, an important addition to any manufacturer's

fleet. On April 21, 1976, Cadillac built what was thought to be its last convertible. It rolled off the production line into the spring sunshine only to be grabbed by Cadillac for its own historical collection. The car was an Eldorado, the only convertible model Cadillac had made since discontinuing the DeVille version in 1970.

Due to the media hype and Cadillac's own PR, demand for the last convertible was so enormous that Cadillac announced a special run of two hundred "last" Eldorado convertibles. These carried a special dash plaque and came with an equally special paint and upholstery colour: white. Everything, from wheel covers to convertible tops, was white. Albino, in fact!

Public fervor was so great that the two hundred were snapped up almost before they left the plant. A further 13,800 "ordinary" convertibles were made, and these too sold out. Everybody who bought one anticipated vast profits – many of these Eldorados never saw a road as their new owners put them straight into storage, awaiting the day to sell.

That day came barely a year later. With the help of auctions – especially auctions – people were paying up to $25,000, or well over double the original price. Why not, some may ask? Everybody thought it was the last convertible, so why not make hay while the sun shone? That's the American way, right? In this case, wrong. Those who paid $25,000 soon found they were backing a loser. By 1980 prices had dropped, and when convertibles started

Top left: overweight and overindulgent, the 1972 Eldorado's interior was opulent in a tasteless sort of way. Cheap plastic "wood" abounded, and while one applauds the saving of trees, why didn't Cadillac opt for brushed aluminum or padding? Facing page: the Eldorado's aggressive front presents oncoming traffic with a toothy grin.

Top: "and where did you get those big teeth Grandma?" At least the grille is not yet plastic. Left: taillight has rubber protection against minor dings. Above: all mirrors are embossed with the Cadillac name. Facing page top: air conditioning controls and cruise control are self explanatory. Facing page bottom: the huge 8.2 liter engine wasn't anything to write home about if the subject was gas economy.

SPECIFICATIONS
1973

Calais (wb 130.0)		Weight	Price	Production
68247	htp cpe	4,900	5,866	4,275
68249	htp sdn	4,953	6,038	3,798
De Ville (wb 130.0)				
68347	htp cpe	4,925	6,268	112,849
68349	htp sdn	4,985	6,500	103,394
Eldorado (wb 126.3)				
69347	htp cpe	4,880	7,360	42,136
69367	cor v	4,966	7,681	9,315
Sixty Special Brougham (wb 133.0)				
68169	Fleetwood scn 4d	5,102	7,765	24,800
Seventy-Five (wb 151.5)				
69723	sdn 4d	5,620	11,948	1,043
69733	limo 9P	5,742	12,080	1,017
69890	comm chassis (wb 157.5)	—	—	2,212

1973 Engines	bore × stroke	bhp	availability
V8, 472.0	4.30 × 4.06	220	S-all exc Eldorado
V8, 500.0	4.30 × 4.30	235	S-Eldorado

coming back, the big 1976 Eldorado staggered and fell by the wayside. Today nobody wants them and, though they can be bought for their original sale price, they normally sell for a great deal less.

All Cadillacs only got minimal attention in 1976, fueling rumors that there were going to be big changes at Cadillac for 1977 – changes that would eventually effect the entire industry.

Cadillac's big news for 1977 was the reductions in length. With the exception of a carry-over Eldorado, all Cadillacs, including the Series 75, had been downsized. After the '73 oil crisis, the growing popularity of European and Japanese cars and just plain good sense dictated GM's new, startling approach for the last quarter of the twentieth century. Not only Cadillacs, but all GM cars, from Chevrolet to Buick, were smaller, lighter and more fuel-efficient. Wheelbases shrank accordingly; the Series 75 was down seven inches to 144.5 inches, while the Coupe DeVille, Sedan DeVille and Fleetwood Brougham dropped from 130 to 121.5 inches. Of all Cadillacs, the Series 75 lost the least in overall length, now eight inches shorter at 244.2 inches – around about the size it was in 1970.

Not only were the cars shorter and narrower, but they had gone on a crash diet and were at least 950 lbs lighter. This was welcome news; in 1976 a Series 75 Sedan weighed an elephantine 5,746 lbs. and a Sedan de Ville 5,127 lbs. No wonder they needed the huge 8.2-liter engine to pull them along – anything smaller and they probably couldn't have got out of their own way! Of course, with all this downsizing, it was logical that a new engine was in order, and it duly arrived. Though still large, at 472 cubic inches (7.0 liters), it was nevertheless a step in the right direction.

New styling was not as extreme as one might have thought for such a revolutionary turnaround. Instead it

At 112,849 produced, Cadillac's 1973 Coupe de Ville was far and away the most popular model. This was the first year for the Federal mandated 5mph safety bumper, which tends to over-emphasize the front end.

followed Cadillac's traditional evolutionary pattern. A narrower eggcrate grille, redesigned bumpers and full rear-wheel openings produced crisp, fairly severe lines, and therefore a stronger similarity to the Seville, which remained the same but for the revised grille. Better yet was the news that the Seville got four-wheel disc brakes as standard, even if its base price was up to $13,359. It didn't seem to hurt sales, though, which totaled a creditable 45,060.

Only Lincoln remained as Cadillac's domestic rival – the danger now came from Britain and Germany; Mercedes sold 48,722 units in the United States – up 5,517 on 1976. Meanwhile, Lincoln tried to take on the Seville with a small car of its own. Heavily based on Ford's Granada/Mercury's Monarch, the Versailles was introduced in March. Sales were only 15,434, but 80,321 Mark V's beat the lumbering, old-style Eldorado by 33,000 units. All in all Lincoln had a good 1977 with cars that seemed as long as aircraft carriers; over 190,000 of them were sold to happy customers.

Nothing much happened in 1978. The downsized "biggies" got a slightly revised grille and raised Cadillac script on the left portion of the hoodface. A new Seville model, the Elegante, was offered in two two-tone combinations of either brown- or black-and-platinum. Brushed chrome side moldings, perforated leather seats

Top: the 1973 Cadillac's neatly executed lighting arrangement, with parking light positioned between dual headlights. Above left: mirror detail shows Cadillac identification, while model detail is attached to the base of the vinyl roof. Attractive interior is streets ahead of the Eldorado's, and is quiet and comfortable, too.

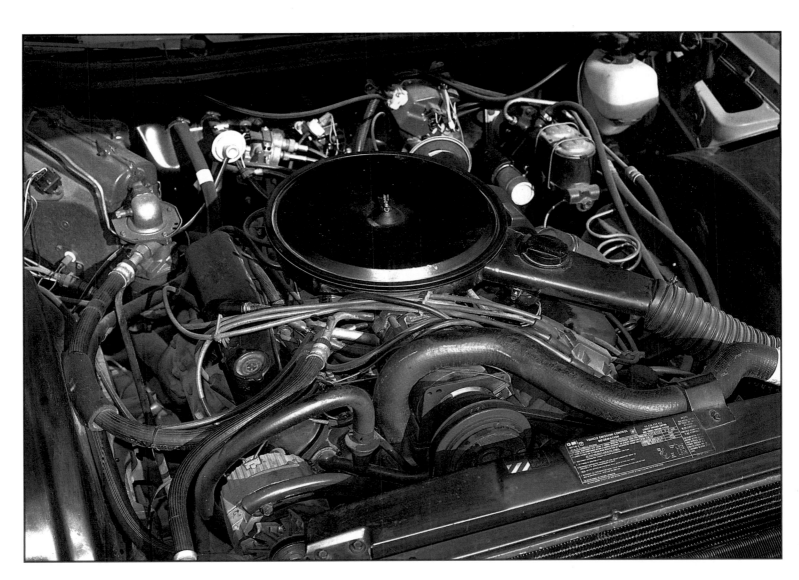

Top: a nightmare of belts, pulleys and hoses. Most owners would need a degree to locate just the spark plugs on this 500-cubic-inch monster. The steering wheel (above left) is collapsible, with a nice thin rim. The wheel cover (above) is attractive, but the phony wood (left) isn't. Facing page top: 1976 was the first year for squared headlights. The first Caddie convertible had appeared in 1916. Sixty years later came this offering, its sumptuous interior (facing page bottom) marred by the use of fake wood.

1976 CADILLAC SEVILLE

as once realized by William Crapo Durant. Nevertheless, a new bustle-back Seville drove Cadillac firmly into 1980.

The Seville also went to front-wheel drive, sharing transaxle, level control, all independent suspension and a 114-inch-wheelbase with the Eldorado, Toronado and Riviera. At least it looked different – and how! It was as though somebody had cut off the rear of a 1949 Daimler limousine and grafted it onto a 1979 Seville – certainly a conversation piece. Offering the 350 diesel V8 as *standard* equipment, the Seville was a car that was either loved or hated and there was no in-between. As for the engine, well, Cadillac was convinced most buyers would want it over the optional gasoline V8. One can't help wondering what went through Cadillac executives' minds during this period. Had they become so insensitive as not to realize most people associated a Cadillac with smooth, quiet operation and a barely audible sound from beneath the hood? Nobody would be happy with any supposedly luxury car – least of all a Cadillac – that clattered like a farm tractor.

And so it came to pass that Cadillac's pundits were wrong: over sixty-three percent ordered the new Seville with its gasoline-powered V8 in 1980. The same unpleasant diesel had been offered on all Cadillacs since 1979, but takers were getting fewer and fewer. In the end, GM realized it was flogging a dead horse with the diesel, as it was a troublesome engine no matter how the engineers tried to improve it. It was unceremoniously dropped and wasn't mentioned again after 1984. A V6 diesel was also tried out, but that proved to be a disaster as well, joining the V8 version in limbo.

All Cadillacs, apart from the new Eldorado, were restyled in 1980. A new Fleetwood Brougham Coupe was added to the lineup during the year and while the full-size cars looked much the same as 1979 models, they actually had even more formal rooflines, full-length upper crease lines, a grille with vertical accents and straighter rear fender lines. This styling would remain with the full-size Cadillacs throughout the Eighties, the only changes being slight modifications to grilles and trim. By 1989 only the Fleetwood Brougham remained of Cadillac's rear-drive cars. Antiquated, carrying an eleven-year-old body with even older components underneath, the Brougham measured 221 inches overall and bore the distinction of being America's longest production car in 1989, a distinction it had held for several years. As far as wealthy Midwestern farmers, gentlemen of older persuasion and those sold on the front-engine rear-drive formula were concerned, there was no car as good as the Brougham, and the sales graph repeatedly showed it.

Production dropped 150,000 units in 1980, primarily due to the Iranian crisis in 1979. 1980 was the first of several harrowing years for Detroit: Chrysler was on the brink of destruction and only newly appointed Lee Iacocca stood between life and death, while Ford wasn't exactly healthy either. Its policy of holding onto King Kong-sized automobiles was wearing thin, even though the public gave the small Lincoln Versailles the thumbs down – it disappeared at the end of 1980. Perhaps developments in the Middle East were having a good effect on the industry as by the time

Europeans beware, Cadillac has you covered with its new, down-sized Seville (right and previous pages). Although a nice-looking automobile, the 1976 Seville hardly scratched the surface of the European luxury car invasion, which continued to grow by leaps and bounds. The rear of the 1976 Seville has a definite Euro feel to it, an attractive design touch added by the wraparound taillight.

Cadillac's attention to detail extends from door panel controls (above) to the liberal application of badges. After all, if the customer has paid for the privilege of owning a Cadillac, he will surely want the neighbors to know that the Seville's engine is fuel injected (above right). Facing page: better use of space gives the Seville more room than the Eldorado, while the fake wood theme is common to both. 1976 Sevilles in nice condition are becoming much sought after by collectors.

people were buying cars again, they were buying cars so radically improved as to be unrecognizable when compared with the cars of 1980/81.

Even with a recession Cadillac's sales did not slump much below the quarter-million mark. In 1981, 252,256 were built, including Cadillac's startling new model, the baby Cimarron. That year also saw a revolutionary engine, the 4-6-8 V8. It was a variable displacement engine which could, at the proverbial drop of a hat, be driven either on four, six or eight cylinders. A unique and splendid idea, but one that was a bag of trouble. Standard in all 1981 models except the Cimarron and Seville (both had their own, unique engines), the 4-6-8 V8 was a sophisticated piece of machinery and very much the "engine of tomorrow" in its advanced operation.

At the heart of the concept was the ECM or Electronic Control Module. This was a microprocessor which decoded input from sensors monitoring numerous engine functions, such as intake manifold pressures, ambient temperatures, rpm, car speed, throttle position and so on. From the information it received the computer then selected one of the three engine choices: the 368 cid V8, the 270 cid V6 or the 184 cid V4. If the information suggested economy, then cylinders one, four, six and seven were shut off; if economy and additional smoothness were called for then the V6 came into operation after cylinders one and four were deactivated. And if outright power was the message, all cylinders operated.

Wonderful as the idea was, the 4-6-8 proved a liability, not only to owners, but to Cadillac as well; so much so that the engine was dropped from all models except the Fleetwood 75 limousines in 1982, only to disappear altogether by 1985.

It was "Cimarron by Cadillac", not the Cadillac Cimarron,

SPECIFICATIONS 1983

Cimarron		Weight	Price	Production
G69	sdn 4d	2,639	12,215	19,294
Seville				
S69	sdn 4d	3,844	21,440	34,115*
De Ville				
D69	sdn 4d	3,993	16,441	70,423
D47	cpe 2d	3,935	15,970	60,300
Eldorado				
L57	cpe 2d	3,748	19,334	84,660†
Fleetwood Brougham				
B69	cpe 4d	4,029	19,182	38,300
B47	cpe 2d	3,986	18,688	5,200
Limousine				
F23	limo 4d, 8P	4,765	29,323	492
F33	limo 4d, Formal	4,852	30,349	508

*Includes 3,685 Seville Elegantes
†Includes 17,250 Eldorado Biarritzs and 2,463 Commemorative Edition Eldorados

In 1979 Cadillac caused a furor with the new bustleback Seville. This is a 1983 model that combines shades of a 1947 Hooper-bodied Daimler with modern Fisher technology.

Top: a slightly better class of fake wood adorns the Seville's instrument panel and doors. Seating is soft leather. A maze of buttons and lights (above) allows the driver to control just about anything. Above right: ten years on and safety bumpers are smoothly integrated with the body. Facing page: with independent suspension, disc brakes, level control and 249-cubic-inch V8, the Seville had good ride and creditable handling.

almost as if Cadillac was ashamed of its "baby." Announced on May 21, 1981, the Cimarron was based upon GM's "J" body shared by Chevy's Cavalier and Pontiac's J-2000. This was product rationalization gone mad because the Cimarron, apart from its grille, interior appointments and teeny Cadillac crest *was* a Cavalier. Everything was the same; same anemic L-4 displacing 112.4 cubic inches (1.8 liters) rated at eighty-five net horsepower, same independent front, semi-independent rear suspension, same everything – even a four-speed manual transmission for the sporty minded. But the price was $12,131. Anybody who paid that, when they could have had a fully equipped Cavalier for half the money, was obviously after the prestige of owning a Cadillac. After all, the J-body in Cadillac guise was the cheapest Cadillac anyone could buy in 1981.

It didn't take Cadillac and the rest of the J-body users long to realize that this 1.8-liter four wouldn't win against competitors in Nohopesville's annual egg-and-spoon race. To try to remedy this, a larger 2.0-liter engine was dropped into the car and though it helped, the Cimarron didn't really start getting out of its way until GM's 2.8-liter (173-cid) V6 was offered as an option. This engine made the little car come alive and enabled it to compete favorably with smaller BMWs and Audis.

Why did Cadillac go for a sub-compact? Given only eleven months for its development, Cadillac's engineers

SPECIFICATIONS
Seville, Eldorado

Engine

Type:	V-8, aluminum block, ohv
Bore × stroke:	3.46 × 3.31 inches
Displacement:	249 cubic inches
Horsepower:	130 @ 4,200 rpm
Torque:	200 lb-ft @ 2,200 rpm
Fuel system:	Digital fuel injection
Electrical system:	12-volt battery, 120-amp generator
Transmission:	Turbo-Hydramatic, four-speed automatic with overdrive and viscous converter clutch

Chassis/Drivetrain

Frame:	Body frame integral construction
Front suspension:	Independent, MacPherson struts, stabilizer bar, coil springs, Pliacell shock absorbers integral with struts. Final drive ration 2.97:1
Rear suspension:	Independent, single transerve fiberglass spring, electronic level control, superlift shock absorbers; stabilizer bar on Touring suspension optional
Steering:	Power-assisted rack and pinion, 16.5:1 overall ratio
Brakes:	Power, four-wheel vented disc, zero drag, 10.25 × 1 inch (front), 10.0 × 0.5 inch (rear)
Tires:	Steel-belted, all-season radial white sidewall, P205/70R14. Touring suspension uses Goodyear Eagle GT P215/60R15

Dimensions

Wheelbase:	108 inches
Width: Eldorado: Seville:	 71.3 inches 70.9 inches Front/rear trend, 59.9/59.9 inches
Overall length:	188.2 inches

Even though it shared the same body and platform as Buick's Riviera and Oldsmobile's Toronado, Cadillac designers gave the Eldorado a distinctive look of its own. Little changed since it went to a new, smaller design in '79. The 1984 Eldorado front-wheel-drive Biarritz (previous pages and right) has good road manners and nice styling.

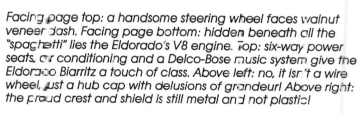

Facing page top: a handsome steering wheel faces walnut veneer dash. Facing page bottom: hidden beneath all the "spaghetti" lies the Eldorado's V8 engine. Top: six-way power seats, air conditioning and a Delco-Bose music system give the Eldorado Biarritz a touch of class. Above left: no, it isn't a wire wheel, just a hub cap with delusions of grandeur! Above right: the proud crest and shield is still metal and not plastic!

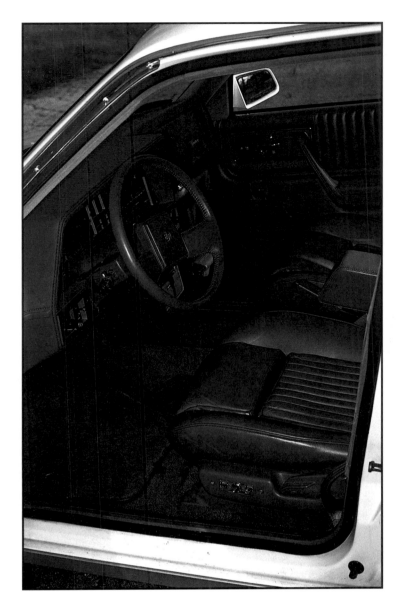

These and previous pages: Cadillac's baby. Born in 1982, the Cimarron was based on GM's J-car, which annoyed a lot of Cadillac customers and limited its sales. Top: the Cimarron's interior imparts elegance not associated with its J-car relatives. Above: emblems denote a welcome V6 option; without it the L-4 standard engine had about as much poke as a hibernating three-legged tortoise. Facing page top: long gone are the days of the do-it-yourself weekend mechanic. It's even hard to determine whether this transversely mounted engine is a six or a four! In fact, it's the 2.8 liter V6. Facing page bottom: Cadillac script and grille are now in weight-saving plastic.

and designers didn't have the chance to hone it to their usual standard of excellence. At the time, the EPA had set manufacturers collective gas mileage goals to meet. Without a car like the Cimarron those goals would have passed Cadillac by, leaving it with a whopping penalty to pay, plus the ensuing bad publicity. *Ergo* the Cimarron – a good idea at the time.

12,376 Cimarrons were built during the '81 model year, which was not bad, but Cadillac cheerfully predicted 42,000 would be produced in 1982. Actually 25,968 were built, a figure that varied by only a thousand or two in the eight seasons the Cimarron was in production. With the arrival of 1989, the pigmy Cadillac was no more.

A chrome accent molding the full length of the body and vertical accents on the grille were the only changes on the 1982 Seville. Production of the well-received bustle-back Cadillac fell over 10,000 as the recession got into its stride. Nor were any changes made, apart from juggling the grille from eggcrate to vertical and vertical to eggcrate each succeeding year, or something like that. In 1982, both Eldorado and Seville got a simulated convertible roof option. This diamond-grain vinyl cabriolet-style roof cost $995 and took the silly simulated world of glitz to its most ridiculous extreme. It was probably cheaper and more profitable than a real convertible, though if the real thing was desired American Custom Coachworks of Beverly Hills, California, offered a sharp, two-seater Seville convertible at a price more people couldn't afford. Who cared when there was a line of film folk to buy the car?

In 1982, all Cadillacs, except the Cimarron and the Fleetwood limousine, got a new V8-engine. Displacing 249 cubic inches (4.1 liters), this new engine had a die-cast aluminum block, cast-iron cylinders and a separate all-aluminium valve lifter-carrier. Rated at 125 net horsepower, the engine had an 8.5:1 compression ratio and digital fuel injection and was destined to be Cadillac's standard-

SPECIFICATIONS 1986

Cimarron		Weight	Price	Production
JG69	sdn 4d (4 cyl)	2,575	13,128	24,534
JG69	sdn 4d (V-6)	N/A	13,738	
Seville				
KS69	sdn 4d	3,428	26,756	19,098
De Ville				
CD69	sdn 4d	3,378	19,669	129,857
CD47	cpe 2d	3,319	19,990	36,350
Eldorado				
EL57	cpe 2d	3,365	24,251	21,342
Brougham 75				
DW69	sdn 4d	4,020	21,265	49,137
CH23	limo	3,637	33,895	650
CH33	limo, Formal	3,736	36,934	350

1988 CADILLAC FLEETWOOD SEDAN

bearer until 1986. British *Motor* magazine gave an '86 Eldorado top marks for gas mileage when testers got an average thirty-two miles per gallon for a trip across Germany.

The Seville and the Eldorado shared this engine and both models remained virtually the same until 1986, when completely new versions were introduced. Built at GM's Buick-Olds-Cadillac-Detroit-Hamtrack Assembly Center, the 1986 Eldorado and Seville were rationalization gone completely mad, just like the miserable British Leyland of old. Those who saw what had happened to BL and its standardization program would surely wonder whether GM was a case of *deja vu*, as both the Seville and Eldorado were as alike as two peas in a pod, with one exception: the Seville had four doors, while the Eldorado had two. Kissin' cousins were the near-identical Rivera and Tornado.

Like almost all GM cars by 1986, both Seville and Eldorado retained their front-wheel-drive geometry, but were given all-new suspension front and rear. Gone were the front torsion bars, to be superseded by MacPherson struts, while the independent rear suspension threw away the coils and followed Corvette with a transverse fiberglass leaf spring. Under the hood, the 4.1-liter V8 had been standard, but was changed for a better performing, much improved 4.5-liter V8 in 1988. Cadillac claimed 9.9 seconds to 60 for the '88 Eldorado, some three seconds better than the 4.1 liter engine.

After years with recirculating ball steering, a rack-and-pinion system was introduced. Four-wheel disc brakes with a built-in zero drag design, automatic self-levelling suspension, the world's finest car radio system (Delco-Bose), a multi-stroke parking brake and an optional Touring Suspension package made both Seville and Eldorado world-class cars – certainly up there with the BMWs, Mercedes and Saabs.

If only they hadn't been so dreadful to look at....

GM's obsessive eagerness to downsize every vehicle it made found the '86 Seville and Eldorado stuck with a 108-inch wheelbase and a puny (for Cadillac) 188.2-inch overall length. No longer six-seaters (or five even), these fifteen-and-a-half-footers barely squeezed four in comfortably – and then it was advisable to have short legs. Basketball players had to look elsewhere for their transportation.

As the longest recession since the Thirties petered out and boom times began again, Cadillac's healthy production record soared to new heights, peaking at 355,752 cars built in 1985. This was pretty good, and

De Ville and Fleetwood		
(front-wheel-drive)		
Engine		
Same as Seville/Eldorado		
Chassis/Drivetrain		
Unchanged from 1985 except steering ratio: 19.4:1 and engine ratings: 130 hp @ 4,200 rpm and 200 lb-ft of torque @ 2,200 rpm		
Cimarron		
Unchanged from 1985		

More Volvo than the traditional idea of a Cadillac, this Euro-style front-wheel-drive Fleetwood (right and previous pages) fits the pseudo English setting perfectly. The attractive rear sets off the '88 Fleetwood. Wrap-over doors hark back to certain wild European sports cars such as the 1963-64 Porsche 904 GTS. Brake light in the rear window became mandatory in 1985.

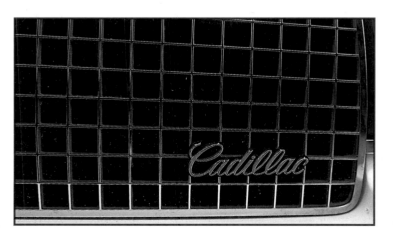

Top: the 4.1-liter aluminum block V8 grew up in 1988 and matured as a 4.5-liter fuel injected unit. Apart from the antiquated, but still popular, Brougham, all Cadillacs are front-wheel-drive. Above left: wire wheel discs lock into place to deter would-be pilferers. Above: the front end looks pleasantly restrained, if a little blasé. Facing page: a plush interior recalls better times, even though much of it is plastic, like the grille (left). Real wood graces the door panels.

demonstrated the flexibility of American tastes. It was only a few years before that Detroit had been preaching the "bigger is better" philosophy. Now they had gone full circle, and were extolling the virtues of "small is sensible."

Of that record-breaking 1985 total, 140,866 of the cars were Sedan DeVilles and Coupe DeVilles, not the old eighteen-foot-long behemoths but all-new trimmed-down models. Now 600 lbs lighter and two feet shorter, both the DeVilles and Fleetwoods, including the 75 limousines, sported a transversely-mounted, fuel-injected 4.1-liter V8, all-round independent suspension, rack-and-pinion steering, electronic level control and everything else as listed for the Seville/Eldorado series.

Gas mileage figures were up and the handling vastly improved without loss of comfort; the boulevard ride was still there, as was the silence of operation. Prices were up, too. A new DeVille cost about $20,000, which was a lot in American terms perhaps, but a bargain compared to a Mercedes or a BMW.

Although these models proved very popular – and for ride and handling they *were* good – they were also very ugly, and not unlike the Volvo sedan. Rationalization had once again reared its head and these new Cadillacs shared everything with their C-bodied cousins, the Buick Electra and Oldsmobile 98. People began to grow tired of paying out for a luxury nameplate only to find virtually the same car, albeit with another identity but costing thousands less, parked next door.

In response they started turning to Ford, whose fabulous "jelly mold" styling, encouraged by the Probe design exercises, led the world to Dearborn's and Dagenham's doors. From the Sierra of England to the Taurus, Lincoln Continental LSC and beautiful Thunderbird, Ford was back with a vengeance, stealing old GM loyalists who could see that each Ford series was totally different from the next. And that is as it should be.

Even though Cadillacs had a price hike in 1986 and the DeVille series increased its production to 166,207, total Cadillac production dropped to 281,318. A lot of the defectors made their way to Ford dealerships. As a result, all Lincoln models enjoyed an all-time high in sales volume, and over at Highland Park, Chrysler, who had managed a complete turn around under the leadership of the dynamic Lee Iacocca, was steadily increasing its market share as well.

Cadillac's ancient Fleetwood Brougham – the one Consumer Guide's auto editors described as a car with little future since most of its buyers are in their sixties – got Oldsmobile's 5.0-liter V8 in place of the 4.1-liter it had before. This was probably a wise move because a car weighing over 4,000 lbs needs extra power to get down to the highway. No matter what Consumer Guide says, the old Brougham is still with us in 1989 and probably will be around for some while yet.

While Lincoln climbed to new plateaus, Cadillac's downsized Eldorado/Seville twins dropped alarmingly in the opposite direction. The buying public shunned them as if they had the plague, giving the same cold shoulder to look-a-like Riviera and Olds Toronado as well. Other Cadillac models did better, even if not as well as before.

1988 CADILLAC FLEETWOOD

By no stretch of the imagination is this a handsome car, but its lines are the model of restraint. The narrow rear window is a Cadillac exclusive designed to give a degree of privacy to the passengers. Taillights are elegant in the Cadillac tradition. Top: even interior lights carry the Cadillac crest and the Fleetwood stamping (above) is actually metal!

Hurrying back to the drawing board, Cadillac cranked out several stop-gap measures in the hope that they might turn the tide. Both the chunky Seville and the Eldorado were given an overhaul which included three inches extra length, crisper front fenders, a raised "power dome" hood, new bumper guards and a revised grille. Sales actually went up in '87 from 1986's disastrous levels, but Cadillac was holding its breath and playing a "wait-and-see" game. This included replacing the 4.1-liter V8 with the 4.5-liter engine in the DeVille and Fleetwoods. Horsepower was more than in 1987 at 155, and Cadillac claimed the same set of acceleration figures for these models as it did for the Eldorado/Seville twins.

Tilt/telescope steering was standard along with almost everything else in the book, yet Teves anti-lock brakes were standard only on the expensive ($34,000 plus in 1988) Fleetwood Sixty Special, though optional on other models. The Sixty Special was essentially the Fleetwood D'Elegance, but with its wheelbase and body stretched by five inches. At 201.5 inches there was plenty of leg room and the car was as plush as a boudoir after a spring clean. Nine optional features became standard on Fleetwoods, including intermittent wipers, dual comfort front seats, and a new electronic cruise control – said to be more accurate than the vacuum-operated system it replaced.

Quiet, plushly appointed and very comfortable – that sums up the Sixty Special, whose ride and handling characteristics were outstanding for its class. With the optional handling package the car competed favorably with the top Europeans. As far as looks went, the Sixty

Previous pages: extremely luxurious and quiet, this '88 Fleetwood might be forgiven its sad quality control lapses – if it was a Chevy. But Chevrolets don't carry $34,000 price tags! Facing page top: dashboard layout is simple, yet refined; instruments are digital. Facing page bottom: thick rear door pillar continues into rear roof pillar; pity the fit wasn't better. Top: the tasteful, luxurious and well-finished interior of a 1989 60 Special. Left: the 60 Special's taillight serves as brake and turn signal lights. Above: another thief-proof wire wheel disc; Caddie goes a bundle on these!

1989 CADILLAC ALLANTE

SPECIFICATIONS	2-door conv.
Wheelbase, in.	99.4
Overall length, in.	178.6
Overall width, in.	73.4
Overall height, in.	52.2
Front track, in.	60.5
Rear track, in.	60.5
Curb weight, lbs.	3494
Cargo vol., cu. ft.	13.0
Fuel capacity, gal.	22.0
Seating capacity	2
Front headroom, in.	37.2
Front shoulder room, in.	57.7
Front legroom, max., in.	43.1
Rear headroom, in.	—
Rear shoulder room, in.	—
Rear legroom, min., in.	—

Drivetrain layout: transverse front engine/front-wheel drive. **Steering:** rack and pinion, power assisted, 3.0 turns lock-to-lock. **Turn diameter, ft.:** 38.0. **Front brakes:** 10.25-in. discs w/anti-lock. **Rear brakes:** 10.0-in. discs w/anti-lock. **Construction:** unit.

POWERTRAINS	ohv V-8
Displacement, l/cu. in.	4.1/249
Fuel delivery	PFI
Net bhp @ rpm	170 @ 4300
Net torque @ rpm	230 @ 3200
Availability	S
EPA city/highway mpg 4-speed OD automatic	16/24

PRICES

CADILLAC ALLANTE	Retail Price	Dealer Invoice	Low Price
2-door coupe/convertible	56,533	48,223	52,378

Right and previous pages: Cadillac's status symbol, the $56,000 Allante. Styled by Pininfarina, this car looks more European than the Mercedes 560 SLC, to which it bears more than a passing resemblance. The Allante comes in three guises – either with a hard top, soft top, or no top at all. The 4.5-litre fuel injected V8 propels the Allante along at a healthy clip.

The Allante's interior is very smart, and plastic moldings are better finished than most. Leather-wrapped shift is an overdrive automatic pretending to be a manual, and there are more buttons to press than in the White House. Above: the Pininfarina emblem has snob value for those who don't own a Ferrari. Facing page top: the multi-port sequential fuel injection system means one injection per cylinder helps the engine to 200 hp. Due to its inability to meet the Federal government's overall consumption standard of 22.5 mpg, the car carries a gas guzzler tax of $650 on top of its $56,533 price. Despite its pedigree, sales of the Allante have been disappointingly slow.

Special had more style thanks to its additional length, but sadly its workmanship left much to be desired.

One Cadillac, though, appeared to be of a quality superior to the rest. This was the exotic and exciting new Allante, a two-door luxury roadster that had a convertible top and a removable, hardtop roof as well.

The Allante, at $56,500 a copy, is the most expensive production car in Cadillac's long history. It is a European/American venture, the interior and exterior design being by the Italian coachbuilder Pininfarina, a company famous for its association with the legendary Ferrari. Pininfarina makes the bodies and interiors near Turin, and once they are finished they are loaded onto specially converted Boeing 747s and flown to GM's Detroit Hamtramck plant. Here, they are built onto a shortened version of the Eldorado/Seville chassis.

Announced in 1987, the Allante was Cadillac's ultimate challenge to Mercedes, in particular the Mercedes 560 SL, which enjoys a justifiably high reputation in North America. To outdo this reputation is Cadillac's goal, but it will be an uphill battle all the way. Nevertheless, the Allante is a high-class, well-appointed, well-put-together automobile that ought to be able to put some lustre back into Cadillac's tarnished crown. All its driveline components are either modified or derived directly from the Eldorado, including the engine and its four-speed transmission. When the car first came out it was powered by the 4.1-liter V8, but in 1989 this was replaced by the 4.5-liter unit. Although it is basically the same as the 4.1, the new engine gained its extra size when it was rebored for use in other Cadillacs. Developing

200 net horsepower and 265 pounds/feet of torque, this engine is claimed to go from zero to sixty in 8.3 seconds.

Revisions for the 1989 Allante included shock absorbers with deflected disc valving and electronic controls that automatically set three different ride modes: soft, normal or hard, depending upon the speed of the car. Wheels and tires have been increased to sixteen inches from fifteen, while Allante's standard manual – yes, would you believe, manual! – tcp has been revised for easier operation. It's supposed to take only twenty seconds for one person to raise or lower it. Hmm!

Only one option is available on the Allante and that is a gimmicky cellular telephone. Who needs that? There you are on a wonderful summer's day, cruising as if on cloud nine, the woman or man of your dreams by your side. Down to the beach you go and sit comfortably, nestled by the soft leather Recaro seats. The waves hit the beach, their foam glistening in the afternoon sun. Romance is in the air – and then the cellular phone rings....

Cadillac originally predicted sales of 6,000 Allantes in 1987, but although the car got off to a reasonable start, sales started to sag by the summer. In 1988, sales were so bad that Cadillac was forced to stop production for two months in an effort to allow dealers to get rid of existing stocks, including some leftover '87s. Word isn't out on 1989 yet, but how many Allantes have you seen on the road?

GM's rationalization program came home to roost with a bang. Dismal sales across the board for the past two or three seasons finally got the message across that people want cars that convey what they are supposed to be. Although GM still leads the pack in sales, its market share has dropped well below fifty percent, an undreamed of occurrence a few years ago.

To try to remedy this catastrophic situation Cadillac restyled and lengthened all its models – with the exception of the rear-drive Brougham, which is more than big enough already. Sedan DeVilles got a three inch wheelbase increase so now they have a 113-inch wheelbase and a 205.2-inch overall length. Coupes remained on the same wheelbase, but gained 5.8 inches to measure 202.2 overall. Styling tried to soften the abrupt, square lines with some success, but what Cadillac really needs is an all-new body frame for all its lines.

According to rumors, and very insistent ones at that, GM has finally eschewed the look-alike car for every division. Chuck Jordan, Chief of Styling, is reported to have said that 1992 will be the year Ford takes a back seat as GM's new designs hit the streets. Insiders and privileged onlookers say 1992 GM cars are breathtaking in design, each separating GM's various divisions into their rightful place. In other words, a Chevrolet will be recognized as a Chevrolet, a Buick as a Buick, and Cadillac once again will show itself to be a Cadillac.

Gradual improvements in all areas, including quality, are Cadillac's plans for the next couple of seasons. In 1992, in its ninetieth year, Cadillac intends to be unequivocally the "Standard of the World" once again and Le Comte Antoine de la Mothe Cadillac will rest in peace, his proud name restored to its rightful glory.

The 1989 60 Special (right) has additional length fender skirts to help give the make an individual identity again.

SPECIFICATIONS	2-door notchback	4-door notchback	4-door notchback[1]
Wheelbase, in.	110.8	110.8	115.8
Overall length, in.	196.5	196.5	201.5
Overall width, in.	71.7	71.7	71.7
Overall height, in.	55.0	55.0	55.0
Front track, in.	60.3	60.3	60.3
Rear track, in.	59.8	59.8	59.8
Curb weight, lbs.	3311	3370	N/A
Cargo vol., cu. ft.	15.7	15.7	15.7
Fuel capacity, gal.	18.0	18.0	18.0
Seating capacity	6	6	6
Front headroom, in.	39.3	39.3	39.3
Front shoulder room, in.	59.0	59.1	59.1
Front legroom, max., in.	42.4	42.4	42.4
Rear headroom, in.	38.1	38.1	38.1
Rear shoulder room, in.	57.6	58.6	58.6
Rear legroom, min. in.	41.4	41.3	46.3

[1] Sixty Special

Drivetrain layout: transverse front engine/front-wheel drive. **Steering:** rack and pinion, power assisted, 3.4 turns lock-to-lock. **Turn diameter, ft.:** 41.7. **Front brakes:** 10.25-in. discs. **Rear brakes:** 8.9-in. drums. **Construction:** unit.

POWERTRAINS	ohv V-8
Displacement, l/cu. in.	4.5/273
Fuel delivery	TBI
Net bhp @ rpm	155 @ 4000
Net torque @ rpm	240 @ 2600
Availability	S
EPA city/highway mpg 4-speed OD automatic	17/24

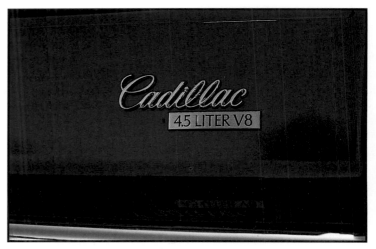

Thick vinyl on the rear pillars (top) and roof of the 1989 60 Special (overleaf) helps sound deadening. Above: unlike Rolls-Royce, Cadillac lets the world know what's under the hood. Facing page top: the 4.5 liter DFI V8 engine that powers the magnificent 60 Special. Facing page bottom: the 60 Special's sleek frontal treatment.

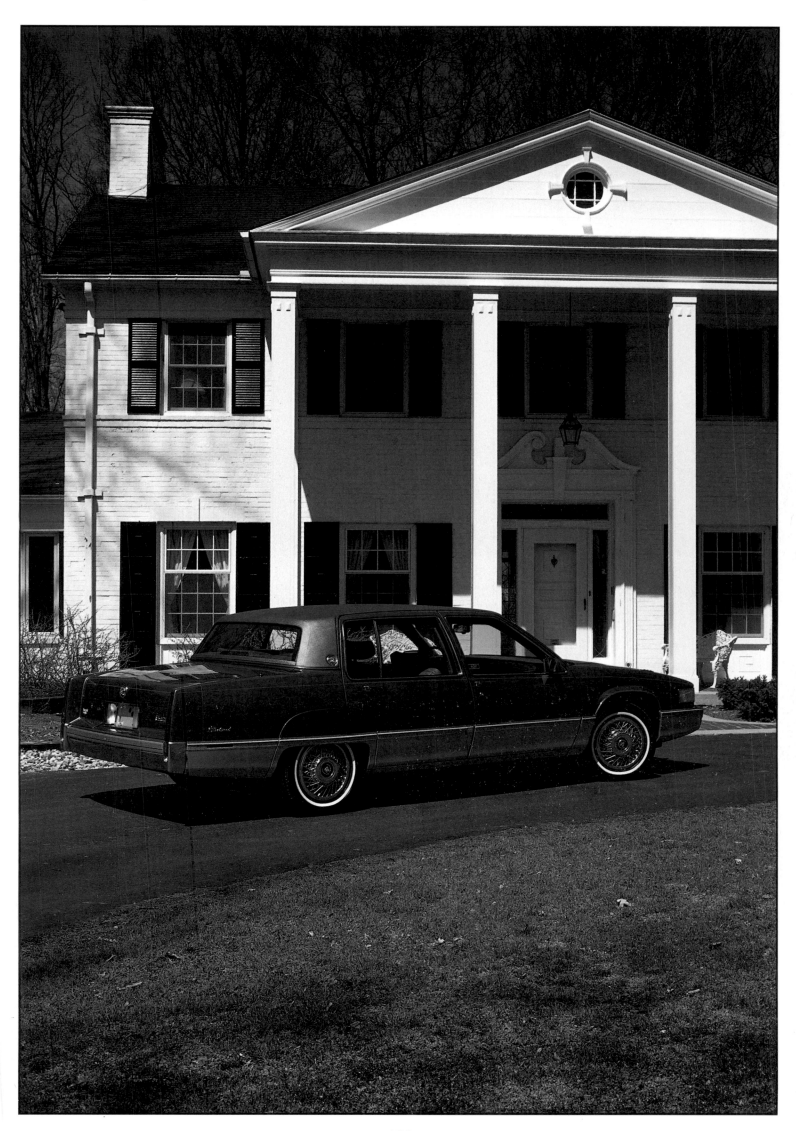